BEN

The Story of Mountain and Glen

By
Rennie McOwan

Colour Photography
By Ian Evans

LANG SYNE PUBLISHERS LTD.

For the friends of the Exodus - Sandy, Ron, John and Frank

"BEN NEVIS". Published by Lang Syne Publishers Ltd., 45 Finnieston Street, Glasgow G3 8JU.

Printed by Dave Barr Print, 45 Finnieston Street, Glasgow G3 8JU.

First published 1982. Reprinted 1983, 1984, 1986, 1987, 1988, 1990 and 1994.

ISBN N0. 1852171 30 8

INTRODUCTION

The following chapters tell some of the tales and give some of the lore surrounding Ben Nevis, Britain's highest mountain.

It is not a detailed and comprehensive guide to the Ben for mountaineers; rather it is some offerings for the visitor or the casual walker.

Some Lochaber tales have been included as the kind of story told in the old houses in Glen Nevis long ago whose ruins can still be seen.

The Ben gives pleasure to many but it is not to be treated lightly — it deserves respect. More people have been killed on it than on the North Face of the Eiger.

I hope this booklet, a gathering together of bits-and-pieces over some years, will deepen the pleasure of the visitor. For further reading, the visitor should obtain these two wonderful old books by W.T. Gilgour, "Lochaber in War and Peace" and "Twenty Years on Ben Nevis".

— Rennie McOwan

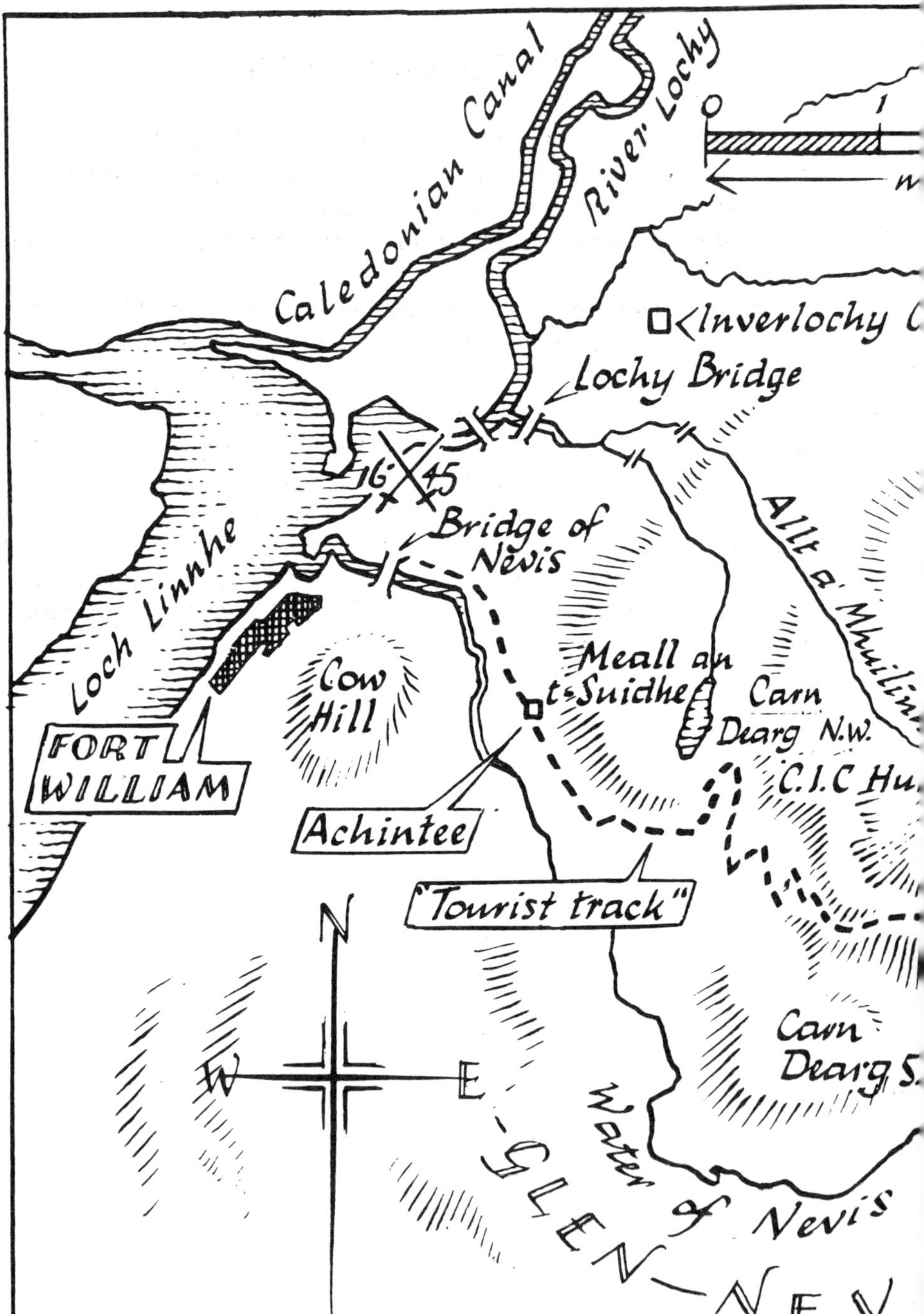

Caledonian Canal
River Lochy
Inverlochy
Lochy Bridge
16 45
Bridge of Nevis
Loch Linnhe
Allt a' Mhuilin
Meall an t-Suidhe
Carn Dearg N.W.
C.I.C Hu
Cow Hill
FORT WILLIAM
Achintee
"Tourist track"
N
W
E
Carn Dearg S.
Water of Nevis
GLEN NEV

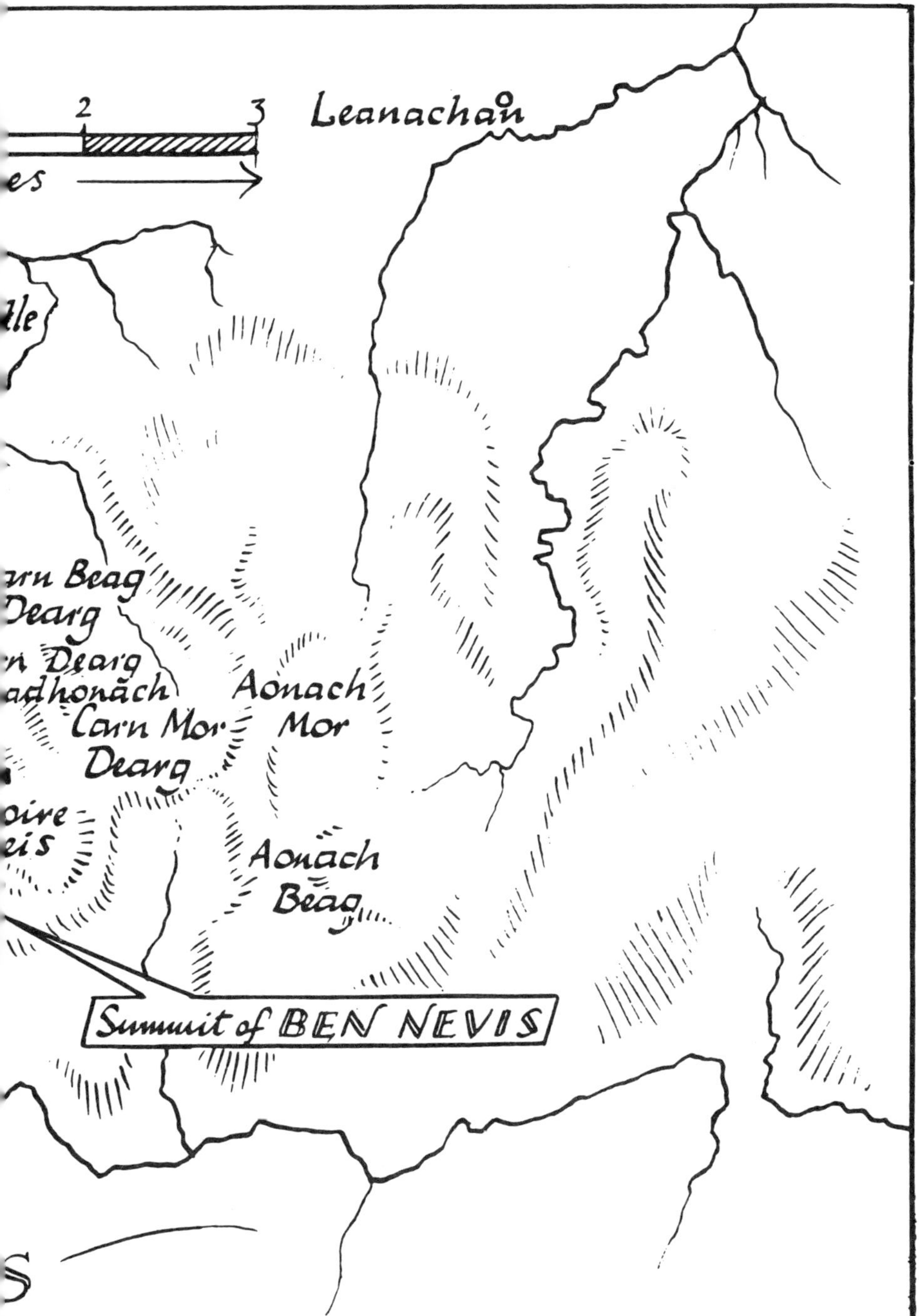
2
3
Leanachan
Carn Mor Dearg
Aonach Mor
Aonach Beag
Summit of BEN NEVIS

Secrets of the Ben

We are really quite flippant about Ben Nevis nowadays compared with the awe with which it was sometimes held in the past.

Some of the early visitors in the 19th century relate that the townspeople pleaded with them not to go to the top, as if it were some remote and unexplored world of peril.

Perhaps they were only trying to ensure that the travellers were correctly equipped to deal with the Ben's storms, wind and cold.

Sadly, the last sight some have seen before death closed their eyes for ever was the lights of Fort William twinkling below, so near and yet so far away in terms of winter temperature and wind-ferocity.

For all its familiarity nowadays, the Ben is not to be trifled with.

We might lightheartedly refer to Fort William as Fort Bill and Ben Nevis as the Ben, but at least it is **The** Ben, unmistakably — at 4418 feet (older maps gave it as 4406) — the highest hill in Britain. (The difference is the height of the actual summit and that of the survey pillar).

Elsewhere in this booklet I have tried to tell something of the lore of the Ben, of its weather, storms, people, climbs and folk-tales.

It is like a venerable old man, sere and experienced, now in good mood, now testy or wild with anger, now smiling benevolently, now white with rage, the Lord of Lochaber and most of Scotland.

Its sheer bulk does it a disservice in that many visitors at its foot cannot fully comprehend its size, and the summer traffic to the top make it probably the most ascended mountain in Scotland, although Ben Lomond must on occasions run it close, but that only tells of one face of the mountain.

The tourist-trek by the old pony track lets the visitors see the easiest way up, and to try to comprehend the Ben more fully the visitor should first of all have a good look at the ordnance survey map.

The 19th-century writer, the Rev. Alexander Stewart, local historian and scientist, who could write pages at the drop of a hat, once accurately wrote —

"Of its particular type Ben Lomond is doubtless very fine — one of the first, indeed, of Scottish mountains, but it is only one mountain, view it from what standpoint you may — while our magnificent Ben Nevis is rather three or four mountains, each equal to Ben Lomond in bulk, and exceeding it in altitude, roughly rolled together into a huge irregular mass, colossal and vast, whose rugged outlines and terrible precipices and headlong steeps impress one with a sense of sublimity and grandeur such as is only partially felt, if felt at all, in the presence of any other mountain in the Kingdom.

"As you make a circuit of the base, a good thirty miles in circumference, and halt to gaze at some selected standpoint in, say, each five miles of the round, the mighty Ben confronts you at each such step under a totally different aspect and you finish with the impression, which such a circuit left indelibly with ourselves, that Ben Nevis is not a single mountain at all, but a colossal bundle of the hugest of Scotland's mountains rolled into one mighty mass, and surpassing all others even more in mass and magnitude and prodigiousness of bulk than in altitude.

"It is the Olympus of Britain, on whose summit, if anywhere, all the hidden mysteries of ancient Celtic Baalism and Druidical worship may be supposed still to linger, and in whose mists and clouds, whether rolling a surging sea before the tempest, or in detached masses reposing in the golden calm of evening, the poetical eye may even yet discern the shadowy ghosts of the demigods and heroes of the old Fingalian song!

"Ben Nevis is in truth the Charlemagne of British mountainland, the loftiest and proudest of his companion Bens — Ben Lomond included — being but his paladins — great, indeed, in themselves, but still only subsidiary and second to **him**, monarch of all he surveys and every inch a King!"

Quite a mouthful, but it's all substantially accurate.

To walk round the base of the Ben means tramping 26 miles, a statement that might possibly puzzle some tourists who walk up Glen Nevis, see pointed Sgurr a Mhaim at the head of the glen, mistake its quartzite-scree top as snow and photograph it as the Ben. In fact, the massive western shoulders of the Ben have been on their left-hand side as they proceeded up the glen.

Ben Nevis on the map (Ordnance Survey Sheet 41, 1:50 000 Landranger Series) looks like one of these jig-saw pieces which, very roughly, used to resemble a hen's foot, with three toes (one going askew to the right), and a spur.

On the left, or north-west, is the 2322 ft. outlier shoulder of Meall an t-Suidhe (pronounced Mell-an-tee, the round-shaped-hill-of-rest or, some say, of the fairies) with its lochan. Its western and southern slopes are contoured by the pony-trail (now the tourist path) from Achintee farm which eventually leads to the top of the Ben and which is joined by the splayed out junction paths from the Glen Nevis youth hostel.

Frowning down on the lochan is the Carn Dearg, northern (the red cairn, pronounced Cairn Jerrak) face of the main mass of the Ben.

But beware, the Ben also has a southern outlier, **also** called Carn Dearg which lies above Polldubh and Achriabhach in Glen Nevis (think of that as the spur of the foot).

The huge curving north-east cliffs above the Coire Leis might be considered the third, askew, toe.

To further complicate matters, the Ben is linked to the east and north by a narrow ridge called an arete to Carn Mor Dearg (the Big Red Cairn.), the 4012 ft. mountain which flanks the Allt a' Mhuillin glen on the east side.

Broadly speaking, for the holiday-walker, the once-tourist, the inexperienced rambler, the family group, or the youth club outing, **ONLY** the tourist-path should be taken to the top, and even then some elementary precautions should be followed.

A walk up the Allt a Mhuillin glen into the Corrie Leis and back, can also be enjoyed without mishap by the careful novice.

Those accustomed to some hill-walking, and capable of tackling some minor scree, and who can use map and compass, might also care in summer to try and climb Carn Mor Dearg by way of the Allt a' Mhuillin glen and over Carn Beg Dearg (the little red cairn, pronounced "cairn bek jerrak") and Cairn Dearg Meadhonach (the middle red cairn, pronounced mee-un-ach).

It gives tremendous views across the glen and corrie to the Ben's magnificent cliffs and enables the walker to see something of

Into the Coire Leis.

the climbing attractions of this side of the Ben. Take binoculars — you can often pick out people on the climbs.

It cannot be stressed enough that when the snow is blanketing the hills, only the expert mountaineer, accustomed to axe and crampons, and properly equipped, should venture on to Carn Mor Dearg or the Ben.

In spring and in late autumn or early winter the steep zig-zag paths of the tourist track can be covered with frozen snow or sheet-ice.

The Ben's north-east crags were once a volcanic cauldron of lava which did not erupt. The lava slowly subsided inside softer material, but its outer-layers changed the nature of the surrounding rocks.

Moving masses of ice then scraped away this softer rock and uncovered the inside of the Ben and left the scalloped and shaped lava, the complicated buttresses, ridges, gullies and ledges, we see today.

It is difficult, because of its bulk, to think of the Ben as a hill isolated on all sides except where the eastern arete links with Carn Mor Dearg, but it is indeed a separate hill in its own right.

The Ben's west and south flank is bounded by curving Glen Nevis which stretches 22 miles from Fort William to Loch Treighead (pronounced Traighead). Down it flows the water of Nevis which changes from a broad hill and moorland burn to a compressed torrent through the 400 ft. high Nevis gorge, so Himalayan in character with its trees and rocks, and then broadens out in the flats of the glen as the River Nevis.

On the south side of Glen Nevis is the inter-linked range of the Mamores, attractive hills which give splendid walking.

On the glen's north side, and between it and Glen Spean and the main road to the north, is the Ben itself, and Carn Mor Dearg and the huge neighbouring hills of Aonach Beag and Aonach Mor.

Aonach (pronounced aonuch) means a ridge, and all four of these hills are over 4,000 ft., the highest mountain mass in Britain.

(Until recently, Aonach Mor's height was given as 3999 ft. and despite its name Mor (big) it is lower than Aonach Beag (small).

Glen Nevis — contrary to some reports is a beautiful glen —

and more is said about it elsewhere in this booklet.

To get an idea of the Ben's immense size drive out to Banavie and Corpach. Glimpses of the northern cliffs, the tallest in Britain, can also be had from the Fort William — Spean Bridge road. An excellent view of its dominance can be seen from the village of Ardgour, across the Corran Ferry.

Two other appreciative appraisals can be had from the Cow Hill, Fort William and the old peat track.

For the 942 ft. Cow Hill, turn off Fort William's High Street near its south end at the Grand Hotel. Walk uphill past the church, turn right, and follow the first road to the top. Go past a housing scheme on to the hill. At the top of the hill, the sides of the Ben loom across Glen Nevis, the Mamores dominate the head of the glen, the strath of the River Lochy runs from the Great Glen to Loch Linnhe and Loch Eil can be seen to the west.

The peat track walk is a five-miler. South of the railway station the Lundavra road goes left, uphill. Follow it for half-a-mile or so until a signpost points (left) to the peat-track. Climb 400 feet, and the mass of the Ben fills the eye. Cross a stile over a deer fence, descend through the woods to the Glen Nevis road.

To the mountaineer, of course, the Ben is an unmistakable shape from many parts of Scotland, its whale-like hump so much bigger than other receding rows of blue or white hills. It is, normally, unmistakably, **the** Ben.

What's in a name?

An understandable, although possibly overromanticised, meaning of the Ben's name might well be Beinn-neamh-bhathais. Neamh can be translated as heaven or clouds and bathais as the top of a man's head — the mountain with its head in the clouds. The summit is only clear, on average, on one day in ten.

Very old maps give the names Bin Novesh and Glen Nevish.

There are many debates about the meaning of the name Nevis.

It has also been written in the past as Neviss and as Beinn Nimheis. The Hill of Heaven is one theory, and many think the river Nevis named the hill.

There is an Old Irish word "neim" and this has been interpreted as 'venomous one".

"The Brave Pioneers"

There is many an argument about who first climbed Ben Nevis, but it all depends on what you mean by climbed.

It would be wrong to think the first men who scaled the crags or walked to the top were the mountaineers of the 19th century or members of the military garrisons at Fort William in the 18th century.

Local people were the first, the skin-clad hunters of the past, looking for hiding places or nests, or simply exploring.

In later years the clansmen also went there, either specifically hunting or for the sheer zest of it. There's a Gaelic expression "Aneil nan Gaidheal air a mhullach" (the Gael's breathing place is on the summit).

Alastair M. Dunnett, former editor of "The Scotsman", put it well in his book, "Quest by Canoe", which told the story of a canoe journey from Glasgow to Skye, first published in 1950 (G. Bell & Sons, London) and later re-published as "It's Too Late In The Year".

Canoeing, pony-trekking and mountaineering in the Highlands and Islands now attract large numbers but when Alastair Dunnett and his friend, James S. Adam (later to be editor of the "Weekly Scotsman" and to mastermind the international Gathering of the Clans) made their voyage it was an unusual event, and "Quest by Canoe" offered sound sense on Highland problems and possible solutions.

Alastair Dunnett wrote — "One will be told freely in Scotland, with chapter and verse, that the kilt was invented by an English navvy-master — that some London tailor was the first to devise tartans — that (although the sword and pipes kept us alive as a nation) our greatest sword-maker was a central European, and the MacCrimmons, the master pipers, were Italians — that no one ever climbed Scottish peaks until some gentlemen came from Oxford in 1860 or thereabouts.

"I do not believe these tales — and I disbelieve them by instinct, without the need for research".

It can be fairly argued, therefore, both by instinct and research that "Lochaber man" first climbed the Ben.

Perhaps he did not strictly scale the long, obvious lines of Tower Bridge or Observatory ridge, although an exploratory scrambler-climber would almost certainly follow these lines at least in part, but that young men had the nimbleness to do this is not in doubt.

The remote islands of St. Kilda, to the west of the Outer Hebrides, produced a race of cragsmen who, in their hunt for eggs and young birds as food, became superlative rock-climbers.

In the late 1800s the alpinist R.M. Barrington, was taken by the St. Kildans to Stac Biorach, in Soay Sound, 50 feet higher than Nelson's Column, where a terrifying leap was made from the heaving boat on to a tiny, slimy, sloping ledge, and with awe he joined the St. Kildans in clambering to the top, precariously 'protected' by a horse-hair rope.

The St. Kildans had, of necessity, become cragsmen in their search for food, and that would, of course, not apply to Lochaber.

Nor, in the struggle for survival, would there be too much time for leisure, but to imply — as is sometimes done — that mountaineering on the Ben began in the 1800s is simply not tenable.

There would certainly in the dim centuries be exploration and trips to the summit in summer by young men, tough, hardy and nimble.

So it is to bare-feet or deer-hide brogues (footwear) we must look when pondering on who made the first foot prints on the summit.

In later centuries, there are several recorded visits. Tourists in 1878 reported 30 small cairns on the summit, some with bottles and messages inside.

Captain Edward Burt, agent and surveyor for General Wade (the Hanoverian military commander in Scotland in the early 18th century who supervised the construction of the renowned military roads) wrote detailed letters to a friend in London about life in the Highlands.

His letters were published in 1754 but were written in 1725-26 and one account told of an ascent of Ben Nevis by some English officers of the Fort William garrison.

A climber of yesteryear and one of today. North-east ridge is in the background.

They set out at 5 a.m., on a summer day but they seem to have blundered around because they did not reach the top being defeated by bogs and "perpendicular rocks".

They reported a change in the air, some snow patches and views of the tops of other hills.

Burt reported in his "Letters From A Gentleman in the North of Scotland" that they considered themselves fortunate to have had a clear day.

They don't seem to have been too accustomed to using compasses as Captain Burt reported that if "condensed vapours" had come "there would have been no means left for them to find their way down and they must have perished with cold, wet and hunger".

An early recorded ascent was made by botanist James Robertson in 1771. He was financed by the Commissioners of the Forfeited Estates, following the '45' Jacobite Rising. He collected specimens for Edinburgh University museum. He was followed by Welshman John Williamson who in 1774 prospected on the summit for minerals. A 13-hour mammoth expedition was made in 1787 by the Rev. James Bailey, Vicar of Otley, Yorks, who was accompanied by three Highland guides, two friends (one a Lieutenant Walker) and two sergeants and three privates from the Royal Fusiliers.

Like many other early travellers they seemed to meet considerable difficulties, crawling at one stage and using a rope and grapnel at others to scale rock shelves. One soldier collapsed from the effects of too much rum and others, too, may have drunk unwisely because they reported breathing difficulties. They pushed a few boulders over the cliffs for fun.

The story of the Ben is, of course, inseparable from the story of British mountaineering in that its crags have attracted all the giants of the past, plus the current crop of stars, and will continue to do so.

The northern cliffs, two miles long, 2,000 ft. high, its prominent ridges and its Alpine conditions in winter, are the attraction.

They can provide rock-climbs of high quality and variety although in summer the rock is frequently wet and much of it is bad, but in winter and spring there are testing snow and ice climbs which have drawn the best from climbers experienced in the Alps, the Himalayas and the other great ranges of the world.

Climbers, too, from many lands, Germany, Austria, France, Poland, the United States, Italy, and many others have come to the Ben, small in height compared with their larger mountains, but have found its classic climbs full of satisfaction and its weather, its snow and ice, and its rock 'technical' problems an exhilaration and sometimes, surprisingly for them, an alarming challenge.

The oldies must surely merit immense respect from modern climbers and readers.

They were pioneers and travelled long distances by pony-trap, on foot, and by bike to get to their climbs.

They were immensely hardy and their gear of tweed clothes, pure wool jerseys, scarves, mitts, shirts, battered hats, and long (alpenstocks) ice-axes, was so different from today's specialised clothing.

The West Highland railway which opened in 1894 brought the Ben within reach of thousands, and the next year and the year after the Scottish Mountaineering Club held Easter meets there, and Alpine Club members joined them.

The last ten years of the 19th century were very much a key period in the development of Scottish mountaineering.

Trends had moved from walking up to 'technical' rock climbing. Winter mountaineering was also beginning to boom, both as preparation for the Alps and for its own sake.

Well-known English climbers, with much Alpine experience, moved north to exercise their skills.

As you walk up the Allt a Mhuillin glen and into the Coire Leis you pass in turn the main features of the north-east cliffs that gradually fell to the exploring mountaineers, Castle Ridge, Carn Dearg of Ben Nevis, Tower Ridge (near the C.I.C. hut), Observatory Ridge, and North-East Ridge, all rising from or above the glen and corrie to the summit plateau.

There were so many characters.

Dr. John Macculloch, born in Guernsey in 1773, who was appointed mineralogical and geological surveyor to the trigonometrical survey in 1814, tramped or went on horseback around the Highlands and Islands as part of his work. He climbed nearly all of Scotland's main mountains. For his trip to the Ben he took a local lad as guide but the guide proved to be a broken reed.

It was August, but it snowed, and amid the swirling mist and flakes the lad began to weep with fright, calling on his mother, and offering to return his guiding fee of five shillings if he could only get down safely and immediately.

John Macculloch navigated him to safety.

Early on the scene was Professor J.D.Forbes, of the Chair of Natural Philosophy of Edinburgh University, who was a regular visitor to the Alps in the days when scientific pursuits rather than pleasure were given as the reasons for climbing.

He is said to have been one of the first to cut steps in the snow on the Ben, between 1836 and 1850.

Among the other 'Alpines' was C.D.Cunningham, one of the co-authors of the book "Pioneers of the Alps".

He visited the Ben in winter in 1882 and 1883, and was accompanied by guides from Fort William.

He surprised them by glissading, a technique they had apparently not seen, whereby the climber either squats on his haunches or sits on his bottom and using his ice-axe as both a prop and a brake skis in a, hopefully, controlled fashion downhill at varying speeds.

On his last visit his companions were the Italian guide Emile Rey, and John Cameron, who had a reputation as the best of the Fort William guides.

Cunningham records that they had to use their ice-axes to cut steps when crossing the Red Burn, and they were told by the summit Observatory staff that if they had arrived on a Sunday they would not have been admitted.

But, of these early years three names are prominent as they are in varying degrees in the over-all history of mountaineering in Britain, Harold Raeburn, Norman Collie and the Hopkinson brothers.

With much experience of the crags of the English Lakes and the Alps, the brothers had their eye on the North-East Buttress of the Ben. They successfully scaled it in 1892 although news of their success was not publicised until some years later.

They also pioneered most of Tower Ridge and Observatory Ridge.

Another giant was the scientist and mountaineer, Professor J. Norman Collie, born in Manchester of Scots parents, who was to have an outstanding climbing career, particularly in Skye. He climbed in the Rockies, the Alps, the Himalayas, and elsewhere, and in March 1894, following more pioneering climbing in Glen Coe, he and two companions made the first complete ascent of the Ben's Tower Ridge.

He also climbed Castle Ridge in April 1895, along with W.W. Naismith and two other friends.

Glasgow-born Naismith was the "father" of the Scottish Mountaineering Club which was founded in 1889, a modest man and one of the first to stress that Scottish hills in winter needed as much cautious treatment as the Alps where he had climbed in his twenties. Because of his Christian principles, he refused to climb on Sundays. His name is commemorated to this day in the names of a series of classic climbs in many parts of Scotland, including the popular rock-climbing route which outflanks on its east side the Great Tower on the Ben's Tower Ridge.

In 1880 he carried out what some newspapers called "the first ascent of Ben Nevis without guides".

Professor Collie, incidentally, has another niche in mountaineering history.

In 1891 he reported the sound of mysterious footsteps in the mist on the summit plateau of Ben Macdhui, in the Cairngorms, thus giving fresh impetus to the old legend of Am Fear Liath Mor, the supernatural being called the Big Grey Man of Ben Macdhui, a story which has gathered strength as the years have gone by while the obscure tales of Ben Nevis witches have almost entirely faded.

Of them all, though, Harold Raeburn's reputation shines brightest. He joined the S.M.C. in 1896, an outstanding Alpine climber, courageous and technically brilliant and he left an indelible mark on climbing history. He dominated climbing in the early years of the century.

He was involved in superlative guideless climbs in the Alps, Norway, the Dolomites and the Caucasus, he pioneered classic routes all over Scotland, and made solo climbs on Observatory Buttress and Observatory Ridge on the Ben.

He reached 21,000 feet on Kangchenjunga in 1920 and in 1921 went to Everest with the first reconnaissance expedition.

The first guidebook to Ben Nevis was published in 1919, and a year later in April Harold Raeburn led a group which made the classic, first winter ascent of Observatory Ridge.

He died in 1926, after an illness which made him temporarily withdraw from the Everest expedition.

Many other men and women should be among the roll-call of names associated with the Ben, ranging from the photographic team of the Abraham brothers from Kendal, in the last years of the 19th century to Dr. J. Graham Macphee, in the 1930s who made over 100 ascents of the Ben while president of the S.M.C.

From his home base in Liverpool he regularly travelled 300 miles to get to Fort William and edited the S.M.C. guide to the Ben.

Standards soar. So many new routes are now put up that they can no longer be recorded except by the most technically minded.

Young 'tigers' take beginners up the original lines taken by the pioneers, and sometimes scoff at the past.

The most popular summer rock-climbing cliffs are now the north-west face of the North-East Buttress, the Orion Face and the Carn Dearg Buttress which overlooks the C.I.C. hut.

Incredible times are now achieved on the gully-climbs, such as Zero Gully or Point 5, and both numbers and standards have never been higher.

T.V. spectaculars tell armchair climbers something of the pleasures of this aspect of the Ben.

So many skilled and hardy mountaineers,....... Dr.J.H.B.Bell, who did so much on the north-west wall of North-East Buttress, and the Orion Face, described by W.H. Murray as "the best and most influential all-round mountaineer Scotland produced between 1930 and 1950"...

Internationally known names like Hamish MacInnes, whose

work for mountain rescue in Glen Coe (and elsewhere) and on the Ben is renowned at home and overseas...

Hamish is a pioneer of climbing and rescue equipment, the all-metal ice-axe, the terrodactyls (a short ice-hammer) and the MacInnes stretcher. He is a founder of the Search and Rescue Dog Association, and has wide experience of the Caucasus, the Alps and the Himalayas. He has hunted the yeti and with John Cunningham formed a two-man expedition to Everest.

As leader of the Glen Coe mountain rescue team he is often called upon to assist his Lochaber colleagues on the Ben whose climbs he knows so well...... of all the writing that has been poured out about the Ben perhaps there has been none more effective than that of W.H. Murray, whose books "Mountaineering in Scotland" and "Undiscovered Scotland" are regarded as classic mountaineering literature.

They can be happily read by both climbers and non-climbers such is their technical excellence by a man as skilled with words as rope and axe.

Several of his chapters are about the Ben. He first wrote "Mountaineering in Scotland" when a prisoner of war. It was seized by the Gestapo. He re-wrote it and it was published in 1947. Both it and "Undiscovered Scotland" boosted a renaissance of Scottish winter climbing, and are still widely read. He has been a president of the S.M.C., received exploratory and literary awards, and was deputy leader of Eric Shipton's Everest reconnaissance party in 1951, and is one of the truly great names of Scottish mountaineering.

There are the brilliant 'moderns' like Jimmy Marshall, who did so many climbs of such high quality.

And there are the less frequent but well-known visitors, who climbed to the highest standards, such as Joe Brown, Don Whillans and Chris Bonnington.

And there have been so many deaths, both on the Ben (over 50 in 20 years) and off it of men and women who knew its character so well; besides hundreds of accidents.

English climber Brian Kellet, who did so many brilliant solo routes, was killed on the Ben in the 1940s along with Nancy Forsyth, one of the most acccomplished members of the Ladies

Scottish Climbing Club.... Dougal Haston, known to millions of T.V. viewers, one of the modern school, successful climber of the North Face of the Eiger who learned some of his climbing on railway walls at Currie near Edinburgh, killed in a ski accident in Switzerland in 1977, Ian Clough, meticulous and with an international reputation, killed on Annapurna in 1970.... Robin Smith, only 23 and destined for a brilliant future.... killed in 1962 with poet-mountaineer Wilfrid Noyce during the Soviet-British expedition to the Pamirs.... and James MacArtney and Dr. Tom Patey.

Jim MacArtney, one of the "Aberdeen school" of climbers was widely recognised as the best winter climber of his generation, and with two companions was carried away by a freak slab avalanche on the Ben's Tower Ridge.

One companion who had untied himself from the rope for a few seconds while he removed it from an awkward snag escaped unscathed.

The death in May 1970 of Jim MacArtney's friend, Dr. Tom Patey, the Ullapool doctor, shocked both climbers and millions who had seen him in T.V. climbing spectaculars. He died in a fall from a rock stack, the Maiden, in Sutherland.

He was a great favourite in climbing circles, composed witty songs which poked fun (but without malice) at friends or the mountaineering establishment, an accomplished accordionist, and a truly brilliant and enthusiastic climber.

He shared in the first ascent of the Ben's Zero Gully, found and climbed new rock routes in many parts of Scotland, vastly advanced winter climbing achievements, particularly in the Cairngorms and on Creag Meaghaidh, Loch Laggan, and completed the first winter traverse of the Cuillin ridge, Skye, in 1965.

If the reader feels the oldies have had more space than the moderns, then one can only say that the oldies were first and that, to some measure, all else derives from that.

The story of the Ben's men and mountains is a constantly unfolding one and there are many chapters still being shaped by time.

"What To Wear and Not To Wear"

Shorts, high-heel shoes, sandshoes (plimsoles), sneakers and T-shirts are not uncommon wear for the Ben in summer but they are unwise. It is understandable for anyone who has gone up and down on a sunny July or August day to wonder what all the fuss is about, but the Ben's weather can quickly change.

An irate R.A.F. mountain-rescue team member told me of an early June day where they found sheet-ice on the zig-zags and put on crampons to cross it. They assisted a group of alarmed holiday-makers to extricate themselves from it (gymshoes and sneakers) but the R.A.F. men were nevertheless roundly abused when they suggested to the party they were ill-equipped.

People do wear all stages of dress and undress and many get away with it.

Mountaineer and writer Hamish M. Brown ("Hamish's Mountain Walk" and "Hamish' s Groats End Walk", Gollancz), tells of meeting a man on the hill who was wearing a raincoat, shoes and an open umbrella.

He also met someone wearing thigh-length waders which, says Hamish, was carrying pessimism a bit far.

If a summer day is really settled, clear and warm, then one can walk, in shorts and T-shirt, to the summit and back by following the track, the cairns and often the crowds, all without mishap. But it's taking a chance.

The sensible will wear, or carry, even in summer —

* Stout boots or shoes.
* Warm, full-length trousers.
* Warm anorak or cagoule, with hood.
* Spare jerseys.
* Plenty of food and drink.
* Map and compass.

If the day is a scorcher, you can always strip off and stick the clothes in your rucksack.

If the weather is unsettled then add a balaclava and mitts if, indeed, you go at all.

In spring, late autumn or winter, the Ben is best left to those experienced on the mountains, and if snow is down then only those accustomed to the use of axe and crampons, should be on it.

Quite apart from technical climbs, those **walking** to the top of the Ben in such conditions should have —

Warm shirt and jerseys.
Full-length trousers and over-trousers.
Hooded anorak, and cagoule or cag-jak.
Balaclava.
Mitts.
Boots and gaiters.
Rucksack with food and drink for the day, plus spares, emergency survival bag, torch, map and compass, whistle.
Ice-axe.
Crampons.
Spare, warm clothing.

How to get there — The normal time to the top of the Ben from Achintee Farm by the path is 3½ hours, plus another two for the descent. Seven hours is also quoted for slower parties.

Leave Fort William by the northern road, cross Nevis bridge, take the road on the right to Achintee Farm where the old pony track starts up the mountain. It goes up the steep side of Meall an t-Suidhe to reach the broad saddle between that top and Carn Dearg N.W. Above the lochan, at almost 2000 feet, the path turns back, crosses the Red Burn (or Halfway Burn) and zig-zags up the scree slopes to the summit plateau. The youth hostel branch joins the pony-track before the first zigz-zag.

British Aluminium supplied the small bridges over gullies.

When crossing the plateau to the Observatory and hotel ruins, and the ordnance survey indicator, watch out for the cliffs on your left as the route passes near the edge and snow sometimes forms a false edge.

There are sundry cairns and, alas, much rubbish on the plateau. Do take your own rubbish down with you.

There are two metal survival shelters on the plateau, and one in Corrie Leis. They are like small Nissen-huts, are painted orange, and measure about 6 ft. by 8 ft. by 4 ft.

Ben Nevis from the North west.

One is on the summit, on top of what used to be the Observatory conning tower; the other, on the plateau, is on Carn Dearg N.W.

Be careful on the summit plateau. If you are inexperienced it is easy to stray in mist from the Observatory ruins and to get too close to scree slopes which lead towards the arete. They are exceedingly dangerous in snow and ice and at this spot in December 1954 five naval cadets were killed when they glissaded (slid) to their deaths. Others have failed to find the turn-off to the arete and found themselves in difficulties.

If you descend from the Ben and cross the arete to Carn Mor Dearg and decide to descend into the Allt a Mhuillin glen make sure you go well down Carn Mor Dearg's northern slopes before descending into the glen as its upper slopes are steepish.

Some climbers ascend the Ben from the head of Glen Nevis, but the sides of the Ben here are exceedingly steep, and the gullies are 'graded' as climbs. This is really no place for the walker.

A more attractive way to reach the Coire Leis and the C.I.C. hut is to go from Achintee or the Youth Hostel to Lochan Meall an t-Suidhe, but instead of turning back to the right to follow the tourist-track upwards, continue northwards across a stretch of boggy ground, keeping almost level, until one reaches an old deer fence. A path is picked up which drops a little and continues in a north-easterly direction and contours the northerly slopes of Carn Dearg, N.W., round into the corrie.

An attractive way on to or off Ben Nevis is by the narrow arete to Carn Mor Dearg but this is a place for the experienced mountaineer, and has been the scene of horrific accidents in winter.

Leave Fort William by the distillery or the golf club and go up the Allt a Mhuilinn glen. After passing the Charles Inglis Clark mountaineering hut a steep scramble takes the climber on to the arete.

At the lowest point of this ridge, and handy for one of the survival shelters, is a line of abseil posts so that climbers can "rope down" when the ridge is iced up. A steep pull of 900 ft. takes one from the ridge on to the summit plateau of the Ben.

At the time of writing, one of these poles is missing and some are loose.

Look out for a large boulder to the left of the path. This is the Lunching Stone, used by generations of climbers en route to the climbs.

But what of the top?

Ireland can be seen 120 miles away, and the view includes Ben Wyvis, north of Inverness, the Cairngorms, Schiallion at Loch Rannoch, the Crianlarich Hills, Buachille Etive More at Glen Coe, Ben Lui at Tyndrum, the Arrochar Hills, islands from Arran, Jura, Colonsay, Lismore, Mull, Tiree, Coll and Barra and South Uist in the Outer Hebrides.

The Skye Cuillin can be seen, the Loch Arkaig hills, Ben Sgriol at Loch Hourn, the Kintail, Torridon and Glen Affric hills, and immense panorama of hill, glen, mountain, moor and loch.

Perhaps the Rev. Alexander Stewart might have the last word (although he does run on a bit):

"What Mont Blanc is to the continent of Europe, Ben Nevis is to Great Britain — its loftiest and lordliest mountain. It is true that Ben Macdhui for a time, erecting itself as it were a tip-toe in the eagerness of its rivalry, disputed pre-eminence of altitude with our grand old Ben, but the last Ordnance Survey knocked the Aberdeenshire mountain's pretensions finally and for ever on the head, and, on the strictest scientific calculations, declared Ben Nevis to be, facile princeps, the Lord and King of British mountains — not merely primus inter parens, observe, like a moderator of a synod or assembly of the Kirk, but primus altissimus literally and absolutely — fully besides, and curiously enough corroborating the correctness of the local traditions that, by a sort of infallible instinct, not uncommon in such matters, had without question or doubt so regarded it for many ages. We may now, then, adopt as applicable to our own burly Ben, the chant of the Spirit in 'Manfred' —

"Ben Nevis is monarch of mountains —
they crown'd him long ago
On a throne of rocks, in a robe of clouds,
With a diadem of snow."

Car that conquered the Ben!

People got very excited about motor cars in 1911.

"I have seen troops get in with the bayonet in an indescribable melee. I have seen cavalry ride straight for the front of an enemy's battery and go through it with all the elan of the hussars of Conflans. Many other scenes have I witnessed which caused a catching of the breath and that indescribably emotional feeling which grips men in time of tense excitement, but that 2½ hours of bumping down the mountain track, within four inches of sudden death all the time, was a long concentration of all those emotions of which I have written."

A correspondent of "Autocar" wrote thus in 1911.

He was describing the first successful bid to drive a car to the top of 4406 feet Ben Nevis.

If it were to happen now the driver and the car firm would be criticised as despoilers of the countryside, but the reading audience of 1911 loved it.

The conquering of the Ben by the 20 horse-power Model T. Ford was a well-orchestrated publicity project staged by Alexander, the Ford agents in Edinburgh. The car was driven by Henry Alexander, Jr., the son of the owner.

Nowadays we are accustomed to Land Rovers and Range Rovers, Jeeps and Weasels, but 1911 was a time when the literal change from horse to horse power was very much in everyone's mind.

The ascent of the Ben was considered sufficiently important for it to be recorded in the biography of Henry Ford, the founder of the famous firm.

It was the ideal car for thousands. Ford founded his giant company in 1903 with the aim of manufacturing a light, simple, rugged car of standardised design which would be produced in ever increasing numbers at constantly decreasing prices until the family car should replace the family horse.

Out of this policy came the famous Model T. and it is claimed that out of the Model T came the 20th century industrial revolution that reshaped manufacturing techniques and put much of the world on wheels.

Henry Alexander Jr. and the Model T Ford in a tricky situation on the way up.

The Ben Nevis task caught the imagination.

"Attempting to describe this feat it is difficult, if not impossible, to convey to the minds of those who did not actually witness the magnificent work of Alexander and the Ford car without being accused of exaggeration. Yet words seem all too inadequate. It is certainly no exaggeration to say that all who were fortunate enough to see with their own eyes the performance of man and car alike are never likely to forget it as long as they live", said the "Motor World".

The author of Ford's booklet, "The Conquest of Ben Nevis", reminded the reader that it might be the greatest feat of its kind ever performed by a motor car.

He reminisced about the Pekin-Paris run which was mostly over level plains and broad tracks after the foothills and boulders of a single Chinese range were passed and with no snow throughout. He referred to the Paris-New York-Paris journey. The untrodden, unrutted heart of Australia had also been traversed by a car, from south to north. There had been car crossings in the Alps, with the average gradient of well built roads being one in twenty or less. A car had climbed Mont Blanc (or to be more accurate, partly climbed Mont Blanc) up the smooth one in eight or ten grade of its railway track. But Ben Nevis was the severest test yet, many thought.

Ford's stunt began when they learned that a regular track existed all the way from the bottom to the top of the Ben.

A reconnaissance of the route behind the Ben Nevis distillery showed that the terrain there was impractical.

The car was therefore driven over marshy stretches on the slopes near Inverlochy and it was planned that it would join the stone track (the present day tourist route) near where a hut known as the Halfway House used to stand on a lower shoulder of the Ben.

(This hut which has long since vanished was sited not far from the lochan on Meall an t-Suidhe).

The entire distance was about seven miles, but even the reconnaissance provoked strong emotions.

A Ford representative wrote: "You cross a field from the road, rising all the time, until you come to a sheer wall of rock, which represents the bottom of one spur of the mountain. You turn to the right, and a path, liberally boulder-strewn, presents itself. This path keeps on rising, as the upper edge of a grassy cliff, for about two hundred feet. Then it turns to the left, rising for about three hundred feet more. Then it crosses a bridge, turning outwards again, and rising three or four hundred feet higher.

"Next it crosses another bridge: you see the bluff and raise it another two hundred feet. After that you take the first — and only possible — turn to the left, cross another bridge, just as plain and uninspiring as the first one, and struggle up another three hundred feet.

"Here, if you were not bent on seeing this counterfeit of a path to an end, you might look down into the glen, where all along the Nevis Water, a Highland farm that looks about three feet long, a Noah's Ark wonder of ordered neatness, nestles under the shadow of the Cowhulls on the opposite side."

He describes the view and goes on.... "the blighting path which you follow upwards again to the left is another two hundred feet higher. Then sharp to the right for another six or seven hundred yards of boot slaughter. Next, round a corner and sharp to the left. There, across a little ravine only about five hundred feet sheer deep you see the Red Burn and the real Ben Nevis towering up opposite .... this so far is only the preliminary.

"You have still another three hundred feet to climb before you cross several hundred yards of rising moorland — the lap of the Ben, so to speak, holding a brown tarn bowlwise between its thighs — and eventually reach the shed which is supposed to mark the half-way distance.

"All we know for certain is that the rest of the path winds up another three miles of eternal zig-zags through loose whinstone screes, to finish in a tableland of snows, twelve feet deep: on the highest part of which stands the deserted observatory and a half-buried resthouse."

He remarked plaintively that the gradient was never less than one in six for the last two thousand feet, with occasional interludes of one in four or steeper.

He noted, too, that only in the latter part was the trail wide enough for a car to comfortably pass. Four-fifths of it meant taking chances, and that not a yard of the trail from the start up to the half distance was wider than two-thirds of the car's breadth.

"So much for the 'regular' track. The whole idea, let alone the enterprise, is sheer madness."

It was discovered that parts of the moor would hold the light weight of the Ford car, and the cross-sprung perching of its chassis allow it "to twist and clamber on all fours".

Ten days were spent in finding and checking a drivable way to halfway, and bridging planks were carried. Three more were spent in driving the car to the halfway mark, and two more over the stones and snow to the observatory. The car sometimes sank axle deep and three times it was pulled out by rope from boggy ground.

The "Daily Telegraph" said that a false turn of the wheel meant a fall which would have caused total destruction to the car and death to the driver.

The "Scots Pictorial" reported that when the path was too narrow to hold the car it was widened, and where rocks barred the road they were blasted away.

The snow on the summit plateau was over 10 feet deep in places, necessitating the cutting of a route before the car could be driven through it.

"The marvel is not that five days should have been occupied over the job, but that it could be done at all, for the difficulties encountered were tremendous."

The descent over known and steep ground took only 2½ hours and was witnessed by many spectators, some of whom had travelled from London, Glasgow and Edinburgh.

When the car arrived in Fort William on the afternoon the whole town turned out to give it and its driver a welcome.

Headed by Territorial Army pipers the car made a triumphal procession through the burgh where a holiday was declared. A banquet took place in the Caledonian Hotel which was attended by local dignatories. Mrs. Cameron Lucy, the owner of the estate in which the mountain was situated, sent a telegram of congratulation.

Mr. Alexander was feted as a hero.

Beyond having the brakes adjusted no repairs or replacements were necessary and Mr. Alexander drove the car home to Edinburgh.

Some praise was inevitably technical. One writer commented: "And lastly, when I say that the descent occupied two hours only you may even appreciate the quality of Mr. Henry Alexander's handling of the Ford car throughout the journey.

"Really, I have nothing more to say save that a word of praise must be bestowed on those factors other than the Ford stability which materially assisted in crowning this feat with success. I mean the oil spirit tyres and snow gripping devices used. For when I say that Shell Motor Spirit, Vacuum Mobiloil, Goodrich Tyres and Parsons Chains were requisitioned you will perceive that Mr. Alexander eliminated trouble as far as possible from his programme."

The driving public were enchanted and some of the publicity was lyrical.

Said the "Southampton Times": "At times, the danger was most imminent, the car crawling along the side of precipices and amongst huge boulders. It is not likely that the intrepid motorist will have many imitators".

The "Car Illustrated" commented: "Ford cars have climbed the Colorado Mountains in the United States, overcome snowclad passes, and threaded their way through the gumbo mud of the Central West. Ford cars have travelled over Chanctonbury Ring and Firle Beacon, covering mile after mile of the bumpy uplands that stretch across southern Sussex. The ascent of Ben Nevis comes naturally in its turn, and leaves us wondering whether anything is left to conquer".

The "Glasgow Herald" reported: "The car has many wonderful performances to its credit, but none I think more remarkable than the ascent of Britain's highest mountain".

The "Pall Mall Gazette" remarked: "It would be as impossible as it is unnecessary to withhold a tribute of admiration for the sterling qualities of the car which came through a test of tremendous severity, literally without suffering at all except in appearance, or for the pluck and nerve of the driver who piloted the car up and down the Ben".

Alexander again — this time driving the model A Ford in 1928.

The plaudits continued:

"The object of the feat was to demonstrate the car's stability and the scientific way it is sprung, which ensures lightness of construction and economy on tyres. This was successfully proved." — "Motor Car Journal".

"The most exciting part, however, was when the driver, disdaining to follow the track, took a series of short cuts over the rocks, the car pitching and tossing in an alarming manner. One hesitated whether to admire more the staunchness of the car or the grit of the driver." — "The Motor".

The feat was repeated by Mr. Alexander on September 13, 1928, this time driving a Standard New Ford touring car (the Model A Ford).

The time was reduced from five days to one, and the previous experience was put to good use.

The writing of the time was less purple than before, but still laudatory.

"Only those who have actually seen its precipitous slopes and majestic heights can realise the immensity of the task which confronts the driver who dares the ascent", said the Ford booklet.

It reminded the reader that the path was strewn with boulders and pierced by ruts and holes, and during and after rain it became the bed of a stream. It spoke of unguarded precipices and pointed out that above the Half Way hut the terrain changes.

"The vegetation line is left behind and the eye sees nothing but myriads of granite pieces of every shape and size. Washed by the winter snows and rain and bleached by the summer sun, these stones are of an amazing purity and present an astonishing spectacle of Nature's prolific grandeur."

The morning was fine and at 10.30 a.m. a large party of journalists, photographers, cinema operators and spectators watched the start.

At 10.45 a.m. low gear was engaged and the car climbed up the lower slopes leaving the spectators behind.

Relays of men had been posted at intervals along the hill at difficult spots in case help was needed.

The model T Ford arriving at the Observatory Summit in 1911.

It had some trouble at the tight turns of the path, but made steady progress, stopping for a time at a spot where a packhorse laden with food had lost its foothold "and slid over the edge to fall 1,000 feet to instant destruction".

The car reached the Half Way hut at 1 p.m.

"Here an enthusiastic greeting was given to the car and its intrepid driver, and soon after 2 o'clock, after a change of oil, the car started on its second and, probably, its most difficult section", wrote a Ford representative.

It cut corners and charged up the stony slopes, scattering the loose granite in all directions. The last quarter of a mile was driven with four passengers on board in addition to the driver.

By this time darkness had fallen, and the car was left on the summit while the party descended to light, warmth, food and congratulations.

The car was unscathed, as was Mr. Alexander, on the return journey, and they both gained for themselves a niche in motoring and moutain history.

"Remarkable story of a climber's haven"

If you walk up the Allt a Mhuilinn into the Coire Leis betwen Ben Nevis' huge cliffs and the opposite slopes of Carn Mor Dearg you will see a small stone building huddled among the boulders and looking very Alpine.

It's worth a look if you want to get an over-all "feel" of the Ben, but it is **not** an open hostel and unless you are a mountaineer who has booked accommodation in advance you cannot go inside.

But even seeing the exterior in its magnificently cradled setting is part of getting to know the history of the Ben and the many outstanding climbers who have enjoyed its gullies and buttresses, ridges and pinnacles.

Allt-a-Mhuilinn (pronounced alt-a-voolin) means the burn-of-the-mill and Leis (laish) probably means a sheltered place athough this word is often used to denote a garden-type enclosure.

Carn Mor Dearg — which is not to be confused with one of two Carn Deargs which form part of the Ben Nevis massif — means the Big Red Cairn. Dearg (red) is pronounced jerrak.

To reach this unique building at 2200 ft. you leave the distillery near Lochy Bridge and cross the main railway line. Climb the hillside to a light railway track and follow it (left) to a small bridge.

Turn diagonally up the slope beyond to reach the Allt a Mhuilinn where there is a dam. Cross the burn and follow a path on the north east bank of the burn. It will take you about two hours.

Another way into this corrie is from lower Glen Nevis. Cross the bridge to the right bank and follow the road to Achintee Farm where the footpath to the summit starts.

At around 1800 feet the path reaches Lochan Meall an t-Suidhe (pronounced Melantee). From there you can descend into the Allt a Mhuillin. But some care is needed.

The locked hut is owned by the Scottish Mountaineering Club — entry by permission and prior arrangement — and was presented by a remarkable husband and wife who with their children were among the pioneering climbing families in Britain.

They were Dr. and Mrs. William Inglis Clark and they donated the hut in memory of their son Captain Charles Inglis Clark — himself a climber of note and a member of the Scottish Mountaineering Club — who was killed in Mesopotamia in the First World War.

Known to this day as the "C.I.C. hut", it was opened on April 1, 1929, and has proven a haven ever since and a base near the rock and ice climbs on the Ben's cliffs.

William Inglis Clark was a chemist who had been active as a mountaineer in the hills since the 1870s. In September 1902 he produced a detailed guide to Ben Nevis which was published in the Scottish Mountaineering Club journal. In addition to mountaineering information it described flowers, wild life, weather and geology.

He was one of the first to regularly use a car to get to his hills, and he was a pioneer of mountain photography.

His wife was also an outstanding mountaineer and she helped form the ladies' Scottish Climbing Club which still flourishes today.

The three founders of this ladies Club, Mrs. Inglis Clark, her daughter Mabel (later to marry Robert Jeffrey, a president of the Scottish Mountaineering Club) and Lucy Smith (daughter of W.C. Smith, a former president of the Scottish Mountaineering Club) met on April 18, 1908, beside a boulder at Lix Toll, Glen Dochart, Perthshire, and declared their club founded.

Mrs. Clark became president, Mabel, secretary and Lucy, treasurer

The ladies club boomed and some of the redoubtable members used to ditch their bonnets and long skirts on the hillside and climb in a variety of makeshift gear.

However, that's another story.

The hut on the Ben "replaced" in a sense a temporary wooden structure, the so-called Half-Way Refuge on the tourist track which was leaky and holed and not unlike the condition of some of the temporary "howffs", the overnight shelters of stone and turf which present-day climbers occasionally build, cunningly using caves or the sheltered hollows among large boulders.

It began in this way.

Dr. Ernest Maylard, one of the original Scottish Mountaineering

C.I.C. hut at the foot of the Ben's great cliffs.

Club members, had one day gone up the Ben by the tourist (pony) track and at the Half-Way Refuge he found gear for an overnight stay dumped by two junior members who were then climbing.

He admired their enthusiasm but thought the refuge was wet, cold and inadequate.

When he attended a club dinner in Fort William he said to Mr. George Sang, the honorary secretary, and others that a proper mountaineering hut was needed. The factor of the estate was one of the dinner guests and he was brought into the conversation. The factor welcomed the idea.

Talk then turned to cash, material, transportation and a possible site.

Dr. Maylard felt it might be a memorial to climbers who had died in the war, and as Captain Charles Inglis Clark was the only son of Dr. William Inglis Clark, he understandably thought of that family and of raising the need with them.

He wrote to the Inglis Clarks and to his joy they replied saying they would erect the hut to the memory of their son.

Permission for building was given in July 1927. Architects Mears-Wilson, of Edinburgh, and builders W.T. Gibson & Co., of Glasgow, were engaged. Less than two years later its six-foot thick walls were completed.

Eight bunks were installed and other fittings including an iron stove. A hut dinner was laid on to celebrate the opening and a blessing was given by the Rev. A.E. Robertson, the first man to climb all the 3,000 ft. mountains in Scotland named in Sir Hugh T. Munro's classic list and known to this day as "Munros".

(The "Munro's Tables" are still revised as map-making becomes more precise. Mr. Robertson gave his total as 283 in September 1901).

Mr. Robertson, a former president of the Scottish Mountaineering Club, prayed that the building might be a refuge to those in need.

He had a dramatic response.

In burst two climbers who had fallen 600 feet down Observatory Gully.

Women climbers at the beginning of the century — insert is Mrs. Clark.

They had seen the light in the hut window and had made their way there.

They were shaken and bruised but after a rest and some food they were able to make their way down to Fort William.

The C.I.C. hut has now given shelter to thousands of climbers and has figured in dozens of rescues.

Improvements were made. The old iron stove, which used to glow red-hot, was replaced by more sophisticated gas heating, sleeping accommodation was re-arranged, and the old paraffin lamps disappeared. The old stove was acquired by the renowned members of the Glasgow Creag Dhu club who installed it in their home-made hut at Jacksonville, at the foot of the Buachaille Etive Mor in Glen Coe.

The C.I.C. hut can take about 20 people (70 have reputedly crammed in on one rescue occasion) and thousands of bed-nights have been clocked up.

There have been minor tensions caused by overcrowding, by unbooked visitors demanding entry, over rubbish disposal, or hut chores, and through its growing popularity as a mountain base.

Some of the best-known names in the mountain world have stayed there.

But as climbing numbers grew, moves began in 1979 and earlier to urge that the hut be enlarged or that another should be built beside it, or elsewhere, high on Ben Nevis, or that another hut be built or obtained somewhere in the Ben Nevis — Glen Coe — Creag Meaghaidh (Loch Laggan) areas. Feelings in montaineering circles ran high.

(The original C.I.C. hut was not without its objectors who deplored any structure which altered the "wilderness quality" of the Ben).

Some objected to the Halfway Lochan being suggested as a possible new site, others to the "urbanisation" of the Ben (if a new hut were built a road might follow), others to mountain rescue dangers and they cited the Cairngorms disaster of 1972 when six children died in attempting to reach a shelter hut whereas if it had not been there, the critics argued, they would have been forced to turn back at an earlier stage and would probably have survived.

The critics ultimately carried the day.

A cottage for mountaineers was acquired at Onich, between Ballachulish and Fort William. It is owned bv the Countrywide Holiday Association and, for mountaineers, is run by the British Mountaineering Council and the Mountaineering Council for Scotland.

The controversy — perhaps temporarily — died and the C.I.C. hut remains the only true Alpine-style hut in Scotland.

The Inglis Clark family were rightly commemorated on May 12, 1979.

A hut jubilee dinner was held by the Scottish Mountaineering Club and a plaque based on an original Inglis Clark photograph of the Ben's cliffs was installed in the hut.

It was unveiled by Charles F. Inglis Clark, son of Captain Inglis Clark.

If you go there and admire the stupendous cliffs which shelter the hut do think of that outstanding mountaineering family whose thoughts quickly turned to the enjoyment of others on the hills when it was suggested that the hut might be a fitting memorial to their son who had himself known these hills so well.

Off with its head!

There were gasps all over Scotland one day in 1979 when it was reported that 300 feet was to be lopped off the top of the Ben.

The debris would be used to fill in part of Loch Linnhe to create a site for a new industrial complex.

The plant would process a valuable ore called Lirpaloof which tests had shown is found in only one place in Scotland — on the Ben. The scheme was the brainchild of the Central Liaison Organisation for Topographical Studies.

Most of this ore would be reachable once the top 300 ft. section of the Ben had been removed.

Because Lirpaloof is rich in high octane molecules (called h — ocs) it can be dangerous to handle so blasting had been ruled out in favour of special excavators.

A three-mile long railway was planned from the loch-side to the summit. A plan to "slide" the ore down was abandoned. To guard against runaway trains the line would have double loops and a kind of "parachute" emergency braking system, and rubber would be used to line waggons.

Engines would be fuelled by peat.

Once the Lirpaloof ore had been extracted the railway would be converted for tourism purposes. Lopping off the top of the Ben should help remove the mist cap that often shrouded it.

Consultant-specialists recommended that the removal of the top could be carried out to a pre-arranged design — the top was, literally, to be reshaped.

A giant thistle-shaped restaurant would probably be built and might be named the Chewchter. It would have a solid rock base, with a revolving centre section.

The restaurant-roof would be specially strengthened as a helicopter pad.

A French consortium, Condue, were reported to be the likely contractors.

Public reaction to the scheme was mixed.

The Highlands and Islands Development Board said — "We are relieved the event has been announced at last — we have

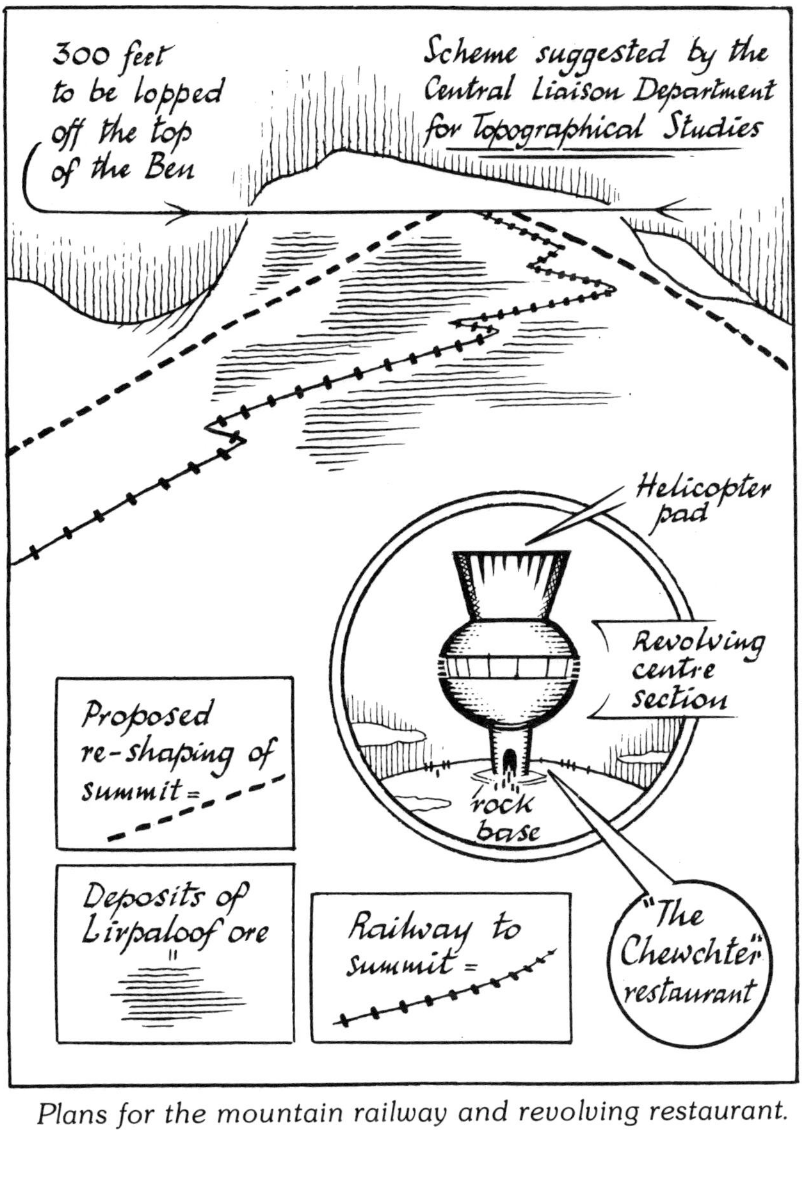

Plans for the mountain railway and revolving restaurant.

known about it for some time... we are keen to be associated with any development on this scale".

The Board said other Common Market countries should be brought in.

Mountaineer Hamish MacInnes said "The discovery of this ore comes as no surprise to me".

Hamish reported that he had taken a metal detector up the Ben and when he saw mineral deposits thrown up by avalanches he thought they were iron ore. "But, obviously, it was Lirpaloof."

"Like all climbers I would be against this project because of what it would do for the Ben. But I suppose there is no denying the long-term employment opportunities that a scheme of such magnitude will provide."

Mr. Russell Johnston, Liberal M.P. for Inverness-shire, and European Parliamentarian, said it was a visionary project.

There was a world shortage of such ore.

He said the scheme posed issues of ownership and finance.

There was surprise and amazement all over Lochaber when this news spread following an exclusive report in "The Sunday Mail".

Then the date was noticed — April 1, All Fools Day.

(Needless to say, all the above named participants were partners to the joke).

" A PIANO ON THE MOUNTAIN TOP !"

The Ben is a regular stamping ground for people doing sponsored climbs or walks to raise money for charity.

Blind climbers were conducted to the top by experienced companions, but not before some controversy arose about possible safety dangers.

Former I.T.N. newscaster Reginald Bosanquet, then 48, collapsed 1,000 feet up on the path in October 1981 while accompanying a group of Glasgow University medical students who were pushing a bed to the top.

Reggie, who was then Rector of the University, an honorary post for which he was elected by the students, later recovered and was able to walk down.

A Fort William man pushed a wheelbarrow to the summit before 1911 (the first wheel ascent?) and then, with his barrow, joined the triumphant procession through the town in 1911 of the Model T. Ford on its return from the summit. It was done for zest, rather than as a charity fund-raiser. A horse and cart has also been driven to the top.

Many people suffering from some illness or disability have carried out sponsored walks to help people with a similar ailment.

One such was by Father Jim Byers, 34, an assistant priest at St. Patrick's, Greenock, himself an experienced climber. Fr. Byers, a diabetic for over 20 years, was accompanied by two teenagers, and they climbed the Ben on New Year's Day 1982 to raise money for a digital syringe pun[illegible] and a blood glucose monitoring unit for Inverclyde Hospital.

Perhaps the best-known of all the 'sponsored' climbers and walkers is the kilted figure of Mr. Kenneth Campbell, of Ardgay, Ross-shire.

He carried a barrel of beer to the top in September 1980 to raise funds for cancer research. The heavy barrel had light-wood 'legs' down either side so that Kenny could rest them on the ground whenever he needed a breather. He has also carried a piano to the summit and back.

On New Year's Day, 1982, he and two friends walked 14 miles

backwards along the Inverness-Wick road to raise money for a special school.

The Ben, of course, figures in car-and-foot bids to climb all of Scotland's 4,000-footers, in record time or to do Scafell Pike, Snowdon and Ben Nevis, the highest mountains in England, Wales and Scotland, in record time, sometimes for fun and sometimes to raise money for charity.

Many objects have been carried to the summit as wagers or to raise money for charity.

In April, 1981, 19-year-old Ewan Milne, a baker, from Goukscroft Park, Alloway, Ayrshire, took his tuba to the top. He raised £100, via sponsorship for his band's trip to Denmark.

"Folk who worked and lived on the summitt"

If you have toiled to the top of Ben Nevis, possibly for the only time, spare a thought for a gentleman called Clement Lindley Wragge.

He went up and down the Ben nearly every day for a summer, from June 1 to October 14, 1881, striving meticulously to keep to the same timetable.

He did the same the next summer, aided by assistants. Although he used a pony for part of the ascent, he didn't have the benefit of the present day tourist track with its easy gradients, but his remarkable stamina and devotion to duty played a large part in ensuring the path was eventually built.

He sweltered in blazing sunlight and almost froze in squalls and storms but he never flagged. He was nick-named Inclement Wragge.

Clement Lindley Wragge was a rugged scientist, deeply interested in weather conditions and forecasting.

He was born at Stourbridge, Worcestershire, in 1852.

As a grown man he appeared to be a bit of a loner. He was tall, thin, red-headed and had large feet.

He ran away to sea where he learned navigation and then trained as a surveyor in Australia.

He returned to Britain at a time when high-level meteorogical observations were being planned in many countries.

The Scottish Meteorological Society were considering building a station on the Ben but there were financial difficulties.

The original idea for high level mountain weather observatories is attributed to Thomas Stevenson, one of a family of engineers mainly remembered for their work in building Scottish lighthouses. He was Robert Louis Stevenson's father.

The idea was taken up in 1877 by Mr. Milne Holme, the chairman of the Scottish Meteorological Society, who suggested Ben Nevis as a possible site. Thomas Stevenson even drew up plans, but no Government funds were forthcoming.

Then Mr. Wragge met Mr. Alexander Buchan, the Secretary of the Society, and made an offer which must have seemed most acceptable to them.

He offered to climb the Ben daily during the summer and to make observations at the top simultaneously with those at Fort William (the town readings would be carried out by his wife).

They agreed, and off he set on his journeyings.

Mr Wragge went by pony part of the way. His route led upwards for two miles and a quarter to "the Peat Moss Station", about 40 feet above sea-level.

There followed a climb to Livingston's Boulder Station, a mile and a quarter further, 840 feet high.

Another mile led to the lochan, about 1.000 feet higher, on Meall an t-Suidhe. Here also a station was set up. Three other stations were placed higher up on the way to the summit. He was a meticulous man, and if he failed to keep his scheduled times of departing at 5 a.m., arriving at the summit by 9 a.m., and returning by 3 p.m., he got very annoyed.

He built guiding cairns, some of them the forerunners of today's well-cairned upper path.

He kept meticulous diaries, and painstakingly recorded the bird and plant life, animal sightings, the sweep and colour of the clouds, and the tremendous views.

Most of this work was Mr. Wragge's own, but he did have an assistant, William Whyte, in the first year, and then two in the second, Angus Rankin and John McDougall.

His 'observatory' at the summit was spartan, a stone hut covered in a weighted down tarpaulin, where he kept his instruments. Sometimes he had to light a small fire to thaw his hands before he could start work.

Sometimes 'tourists' interfered with his equipment.

The severity of the Ben's weather was shown when, in late August, gales forced him to crawl across the plateau.

During the Great Storm of October 14, 1881 — which caused national havoc — he was beaten back.

The Scottish Meteorological Society awarded him their gold medal, an award he richly deserved.

Perhaps his individualistic outlook and drive made him a difficult man to work with. but whatever the reason he was to be

n Nevis reflected in the waters of the Caledonian Canal Basin, Corpach.

ı Nevis and Glen Nevis from the slopes of Mullach nan Coirean.

Sgurr A'Mhaim behind pines in Glen Nevis.

n Nevis from Aonach Beag.

Closer view of Sgurr A 'Mhaim

First of the Autumn snows on Sgurr A'Mhaim, seen from the banks of the river Nevis.

Clement Lindley Wragge offered to climb the Ben daily.

bitterly disappointed by not being appointed supervisor at the new summit observatory which was officially opened on October 17, 1883.

His assistants, William Whyte and Angus Rankin, carried on the work.

Mr. Wragge returned to Australia in 1884. He set up a Meteorological Observatory there, and became Government Meteorologist for Queensland.

High-level stations were set up on Mount Wellington and elsewhere and he undoubtedly drew on his Ben Nevis experience when advising on materials and instruments.

He died in Auckland in 1922, and rightly enjoys a revered place in the annals of the Ben.

The ruins of the Observatory — which was to operate for 21 years — are in a real sense a monument to him.

It was the first mountain-top observatory in Europe.

Money was tight when it was built and there was a public appeal for funds. Queen Victoria gave £50.

A bridle path to transport building materials to the top was constructed starting at Achintee (the present-day 'tourist' track).

There was a toll of one shilling for walkers and three shillings (later five) for those on pony-back.

Permits could be obtained from a shop in Fort William, and from a path-maintenance man based at a 'half-way' hut above Lochan Meall an t-Suidhe.

The first observatory building was later found to be too small. The ferocity of Ben Nevis weather can be judged by the fact that the outside walls were 10-13 feet thick at the base.

There was one main livingroom, 13 feet square and three small bedrooms opening off, plus a store-room and a coal cellar.

The builder was Fort William contractor James McLean and the first superintendent a Mr. R.T. Omond. His chief assistant and eventual successor was Mr. Angus Rankin, who had assisted the tireless Mr. Wragge.

The official opening on Wednesday, October 17, 1883, was declared a holiday in Fort William. At 9 a.m., a procession of officials, councillors, community leaders and others set off from the Alexandra Hotel to go up the pony track, headed by a piper.

The ladies in the party were led by the landowner, Mrs. Cameron Campbell, riding a white garron.

It rained low down, with snow showers higher up.

The party were received by the architect and by Mr. Omond, and hot drinks, speeches and cheers heralded the start of 21 years work which was to be admired and copied in many European countries; and which is still valued today.

Day and night, summer and winter, temperature readings and other observations were carried out at the summit in conjunction with the one opened at sea level in 1890 and also, from time to time, midway up the mountain at a temporary building during some summers.

Sea-level readings were taken by a local teacher until the ground-base observatory was built in Fort William.

The staff often had to dig themselves out of deep snow drifts before starting work and the continuity of their researches was sometimes broken.

A second 'wing' was added, with an office-cum-laboratory, two additional bedrooms, a visitors room, and a tower equipped with self-recording gear and a doorway more suited to Nevis storms.

The outer walls were of granite, the inside double walls were of wood covered in felt. The roof was lead.

The Observatory was connected first by telegraph, and then by phone, to the Fort William Post Office and also with its sister-station there.

Two months was the normal summit 'shift' — after that, there was an exchange with a colleague on the ground.

The staff had fresh food in summer, plus tinned food for nine months taken up in summer by horses, the goods being carried in panniers. The horses, in good weather, made almost daily ascents, Sundays excepted. Coke for fuel was carried up the same way. Frozen mutton was hung outside the walls.

The site became a popular visitors attraction. The staff of four were serviced by a fifth, based in Fort William, who was responsible for the condition of the path, for stores and mail.

In summer, pony-loads of supplies and mail went up almost daily. In winter severe weather sometimes meant gaps of several days or weeks.

Water was obtained from a small spring on the south-east side of the plateau, a little lower than the Observatory. If the spring dried up, the horses brought casks of water which filled large pans in the kitchen. In winter, snow was melted.

A Fort William hotelier built a wooden 'Observatory Hotel' nearby to cater for walkers and those who wanted to see the sun rise.

It became fashionable for a time to ascend by pony — the charge for a guide and steed was 21 shillings. Lunch cost three shillings and bed-and-breakfast 10 shillings.

The changes in the Ben's weather is shown by a tale of Observatory staff changing shifts. The sky was almost cloudless, the sun shone (although it was February) and there was no wind. Before they go halfway, a gale and snow storm blew up, and they had to cut steps in the iced-up path. They were driven back to Fort William.

The first staff spent much of their time in winter simply trying to keep their doorway clear of snow.

One of the staff in September heard a shout in the night and found two foreign ladies, both soaked, sitting precariously on a ledge above the cliffs. He guided them to the hotel and safety.

The Observatory mail-runner was lucky to survive one day in February when he lost his way in mist, and was later found by searchers.

In June 1895 the Observatory was struck by lightning in a storm. Snow and hail fell. Flame and smoke burst from the telegraph instrument. The cook, who had been in the office, was knocked unconscious. In the kitchen a flour tin, a box and a picture were hurled across the room. The interior woodwork was set on fire.

Sometimes, if gales were severe, the staff roped themselves together if they had to leave the Observatory.

They were greatly distressed one September when Mr. Duncan Macgillivray, the telephone clerk, was found dead on the slopes of the Ben near the Observatory. He had descended to take part in the annual shooting competition of the Cameron Volunteers at Fort William on a Friday. Returning on the Sunday, he collapsed and died, unheard and unseen, by his colleagues nearby.

The staff reported many phenomena of weather shapes and colours. They saw an enlarged "Brochon Spectre" called "The Glories" in which in winter, when the sun was low, the shadow of a person on the cliff was thrown clear of the rocks into the glen below.

In bright winter weather, and with swirling mist in the glen and corrie, the person saw his "head" surrounded by coloured rings. The "glories" were less frequent in summer but they were seen. Moon and sun "fog-bows" were also seen, curving and coloured bands of mist like rainbows. Mock suns, halos, and St. Elmo's fire ("fire" displays on the lightning rods and other objects) were also recorded.

The aurora borealis and feather 'crystals' of ice were admired. An earthquake was recorded in 1884. "Silver thaw", rain falling when the temperature was below freezing, and turning into ice, caused much inconvenience to the staff by affecting instruments.

Ferocious storms sometimes prevented the staff leaving the Observatory to check instruments, and one man who left the conning tower' door in storm and deep snow without grasping a guide rope only got back in, unscathed, with the help of his colleagues and totally pastered in snow and ice.

Cornices (false edges, like icing on a cake) at the edge of the cliffs measured 15 to 25 feet, and snow on the summit was from 12 to 14 feet deep.

The staff made the most of winter sports. They made sledges, and one with a sail almost took its rider over the cliffs. Snow-shoes and skis were also used, and an outdoor ping-pong table was made of frozen snow. Snow holes were dug just for the fun of it. Other pastimes included wood carving, playing the pipes, violin, flute, mandolin and accordion. They also skated on a rink made by pouring water on to a tarpaulin where it froze. One Fort William gentleman even rigged up a gramophone at the low-level phone so that those above at the Observatory could listen in and enjoy the recital.

Quoits, using rope-rings, was played on the roof of the Observatory and visitors sometimes joined in.

They also — alarmingly to modern ears — hurled large boulders over the cliffs so they could hear them rumble and crash into the glen below.

In October, 1899, a dog which had fallen over the cliffs was rescued from a ledge after six days. It was taken to the Observatory where it recovered.

The staff often caught an ailment called "the Ben Nevis cough" when they descended from the summit to Fort William. It was a kind of 'flu, with a sore throat and cough. The answer appeared to lie in the fact that the summit cold killed many germs.

A paper read to the British Medical Association suggested that, in some circumstances, tuberculosis might be treated by 'high level residence'. It was suggested a sanitorium might be established on the Ben's summit.

Visitors calling at all hours sometimes irritated the staff, but they offered hospitality to most callers. Their records show visits by age-groups as diverse as an 83-year-old man and a three-months-old-baby and its mother.

A pendulum clock in the summit Observatory is reputed to be one taken by Captain Cook on his voyages and also used by Maskelyne, then Astronomer-Royal, to carry out his pendulum experiment on Schiehallion in the determination of the earth's mass.

The Ben had a strong effect on exploration. Among the volunteer guest-scientists who stayed for some winter months in 1900 were two Royal Navy officers, Michael Barne and Charles Rawson Royds. Barne was studying magnetic data and Royds meteorology. They both went with Captain Scott's "Discovery" expedition to the Antartic in 1901, as did a former Nevis observatory cook.

Visiting student-staff at the Observatory included C.T.R.Wilson, from Glencorse, Edinburgh, who was later to become a Nobel prize winner for his work in the development of nuclear physics. The optical phenomena shown when the sun shone on the clouds influenced his thoughts towards imitating them in the laboratory which led to 40 years of tracking atoms.

A plaque to C.T.R. Wilson was unveiled at the Observatory ruins by his daughter Rosamund on July 27, 1969.

Financial storms, not natural ones, were to end the Observatory's life. Despite public outcries, which have rumbled to this day, public funds were not forthcoming and it could not continue.

On October 1, 1904, the Observatory was finally shut down.

The summit 'hotel' continued for a time and then it, too, died and crumbled away.

There are still two memorials to the Observatory, other than the ruins. One is Gardyloo Gully, one of the hardest present-day ice climbs on the Ben. It is so named because rubbish from the Observatory and the hotel was sometimes heaved over the cliffs, in the manner of Edinburgh housewives of past centuries who emptied their slops from upper windows into the street to cries of "Gardez L'Eau!"

The other is Observatory Ridge, one of the best-known rock-features of the Ben.

And the Nevis storms, now unrecorded, continue to rage.

Snowstorms on a sunny day...

A sunny day in Fort William can also be a snow storm day on the top of the Ben.

The **average** summit temperature is one degree **below** freezing. A few hundred feet higher and the Ben would have a glacier on top.

Wind and cold together can be killers, and the Ben's summit temperatures are similar in winter to Arctic Norway.

A survey report by P.A. Smithson & H. Baldwin, reported in the October 1978 edition of the magazine "Climber & Rambler", put the Ben top of the "wind-chill" league.

The mountain lies in the storm-track of North Atlantic hurricanes, and many storms on the Ben (sometimes when weather is calm at sea level) can reach hurricane force with winds of 100 m.p.h. and gusts of 150 m.p.h. or over.

Clement Wragge called the top area of the Ben "the plateau of storms".

The old Observatory records showed that from 1883 to 1904 there was an average of 261 gales a year.

The height of the Ben often means that atmospheric condensation gives it a cloud cap when other hills are clear.

Clement Wragge reported that the wettest year was 1898 (240.12 inches). The wettest month was December 1900 (48.34 inches). Only in April, May and June was the monthly rainfall under 10 inches. The annual rainfall is normally 157 inches.

There is, on average, about two hours of bright sunshine a day.

Huge false edges of snow called cornices can form on the rocks and ledges in winter and spring.

"The Great Race"

Many Highland games have a hill-race up the sides of the nearest knoll, or to the top, and many well-known mountains now have races, organised and formal, to their summit-cairn.

It is an ancient custom and long before the official Ben Nevis race began in 1895 there would be young men, in a spirit of informal challenge, who would for fun, or a wager, race one another to the top.

But there is no race quite like that on the Ben. It is steep and rough, starts almost from sea level, has a length of over 10 miles and is regarded as the hardest of its kind in Britain.

Before it reached its present formalised and controlled state, there are accounts of both young and old clocking up remarkable times.

A Mr. D. Forbes, of Fort William, reached the summit of the Ben from Fort William in three hours and danced a Highland fling on the roof of the observatory. He was 80.

Bearing in mind that many younger walkers took considerably longer it was a highly commendable effort.

The local people turn out in large numbers to cheer today's runners on the first Saturday in September.

In 1895, William Swan, a local man, panted his way from the Old Post Office to the summit and back in 2 hours 41 minutes.

He temporarily lost his crown to Leith's William MacDonald (2 hours, 27 minutes) two years later but regained it soon after by knocking off another seven minutes.

Willie Swan left from the old post office in the High Street which was replaced two years later when Willie MacDonald made his bid, and his is therefore regarded as an unbroken record.

Older citizens can take comfort in the fact that in 1897, Colonel Spencer Acklom, of the Connaught Rangers regiment, did it in 2 hours, 55 minutes. He was then aged 53, and was said to have had much experience with his regiment in the foothills of the Himalayas.

Variations of the race sprang up, one from Banavie and another from Achintee farm to the summit only.

William MacDonald clocked up another 2 hours, 18 minutes in 1899, but in 1903 Ewan Mackenzie, the Observatory roadman, did an amazing 2 hours, 10 minutes. Ewan also won the Achintee-to-the-summit race.

The first competitive race, as distinct from an individual, timed, runner, was organised by a local hotel keeper who offererd gold medals to the first ten home. They began on theAchintee road and a shotgun was fired instead of today's starting pistol.

Hugh Kennedy, a gamekeeper, achieved 2 hours, 41 minutes, but the race was now longer in length.

When the summit Observatory closed in 1904 (and also possibly because a contestant in 1903 collapsed and remained unconscious for ten hours) the race was discontinued.

However, in 1934 it was restarted from the New Post Office.

The Second World War and its aftermath caused further interruptions, but in 1943 it all got going again.

Heavy traffic in the town meant the starting point being switched to the King George V playing field, and in 1971 it was transferred to New Town Park.

It is now a mammoth event, very well organised by the Ben Nevis Race Association, and drawing over 400 athletes, including women, from all over Britain.

The Lochaber Mountain Rescue Team supervise safety arrangements and in 1981 they expressed their concern about growing numbers.

The field now includes sprinters in with a chance for first place and toilers who only want to complete the course.

With a strung-out field the rescue-team members were concerned that in mist, and with such numbers, that an injured runner could easily be missed

In 1980 appalling weather caused the race to be cancelled for the first time, thus robbing the legendary Mr. Eddie Campbell of his opportunity to take part in 30 races in a row.

He has won the race three times.

The rescue-team rope off the top of Gardyloo gully on the summit-plateau, and extra officials are now on duty. The organisers have the right to restrict numbers and to refuse entry from any runner they consider to be not experienced enough.

There are medals for the first ten men home, seven team prizes and nine special prizes. Each runner who completes the course within a set time received a competion certificate.

Take a look at these times.

Duncan MacIntyre, a local butcher and later to be Honorary President of the Race Association, won the first race from the King George V Park in 1943 with a time of 2 hours, 4 minutes, 30 seconds.

Peter Hall, of Barrow, who has won the race four times, has clocked 1 hour, 38 minutes, 50 seconds.

Harry Walker, of Blackburn Harriers, was the first to break the 1½ hour (by 22 seconds) from the new park.

Dave Cannon, of Kendal A.C. - five times winner to date - has achieved an incredible one hour, 26 minutes, 55 seconds.

Billy Bland, from the famous Lake District fell-running family, came within one second of breaking that in 1978. Bob Whitfield, of Kendal, won in 1981 with 1 hour, 26 minutes, 57 seconds, three seconds outside the record.

There have been outstanding women as well although they were not accepted as official entrants until very recently.

There have been outstanding women as well.

In 1909 Miss Elizabeth Wilson-Smith, of Duns, made the summit from the post office in one hour, 51 minutes.

In 1955, Kathleen Connochie, the 16-year-old daughter of a Fort William doctor completed the round in 3 hours, two minutes, from the King George V playing field, an outstanding achievement.

Ros Coats, of the Lochaber club, clocked 1 hour, 44 minutes in 1981 to set a new record in the ladies event and to finish 51st in the overall field of 350.

The Ben Nevis race is special, and by the time you read this new records may well have been set.

"Pebbles and Boulders"

Tales of witches abound in the Highlands and Ben Nevis was said to be the refuge of one of the best-known, the Cailleach Bheur.

She is reputed to have kept a beautiful maiden prisoner, but her son fell in love with the maiden and they made plans to escape and to marry.

The Cailleach Bheur, in a bid to prevent them and to keep them apart, raised several storms of great ferocity.

But they got away and, presumably, lived happily ever after.

In past years a small plaque saying "Ben Nevis 4406 feet" and "Erected by the Scottish Mountaineering Club" used to be attached to the summit cairn.

It has now gone, and there is a strong wave of opinion nowadays that plaques, signs, unnecessary cairns, are wrong and unsightly and should be removed. The summit has far too much junk.

There are no signs left now, but the half-way point of the tourist (pony) track was once the site of a hut where the walker bought a one-shilling toll ticket which was marked "Ben Nevis Summit" when the walker reached the top.

For many years Ben Macdhui (now 1309 metres) in the Cairngorms, was thought to be Britain's highest mountain, but arguments did rage.

Welshman Thomas Pennant, 18th century traveller, scientist and writer, was only 56 feet out in 1769 when he measured the height of Ben Nevis.

The Rev. Dr. George Skene Keith visited the main Cairngorm peaks when modern triangulation was first used in mapmaking in Scotland.

He calculated the height of Ben MacDhui, and gave his barometer to his son with instructions that he was to climb Ben Nevis. As a result Nevis moved to the top of the British height league.

As sometimes happens in such cases, various suggestions were locally made to 'up' Ben Macdhui. A huge cairn was suggested and a 100 ft. burial vault but these symptoms of hurt local pride came to nothing.

When ice coated the surface of Loch Meall an t-Suidhe in past years Fort William curlers carried their gear up for curling contests, surely one of the highest outdoor rinks in Britain.

In common with some other Scottish mountains, suggestions have been made that a light railway should be constructed to the top of the Ben. The route was surveyed, but in 1900 it happily came to nothing when one of the landowners, Lord Abinger, raised objections.

The name Ben Nevis or Nevis has been exported to hills and other sites in many parts of the globe. One such, well-known to many Servicemen, is a 1600 ft. hill in the New Territories of Hong Kong, just under a mile from the Chinese border.

A sewing machine and a motorbike are among the goods taken to the top and photographed, working, for commercial purposes.

In past centuries the south side of Ben Nevis was said to have been covered in a large pine forest which extended from the western braes of Lochaber to Blackwater and Rannoch Moor and which was burned to expel wolves.

The poet, Keats, when he had less than three years to live and was aged 23, visited Scotland in 1818 and climbed Ben Nevis. He and a companion, Charles Brown, walked over 600 miles from Lancaster, staying in lodgings and inns and visiting Burns' sites in Ayrshire, as well as Loch Lomond, Mull and Iona, Loch Ness, and other sites and eventually halting at Inverness. He reported of his visit to the Ben that he was preceded up by the fattest woman in Inverness-shire.

Among the many distinguished visitors who have toiled to the top was the Africa explorer Mungo Park who went up with his brother-in-law James Dickson.

Bonfires have been built on the Ben since the distant past. One of the most memorable was in 1842 when Queen Victoria made her first Scottish tour. Local people carried wood, rubbish and tar barrels to the top, a harder task than more modern times when helicopters have been used on Scottish hills.

The fires flared up again on Queen Victoria's Diamond Jubilee on June 22, 1897. It was hoped to ignite the fire from London by means of the Observatory telegraph wire but the bid failed. It snowed and there was two-feet underfoot! The Cameron Volunteers, in full dress, fired a salute and a piper played the national anthem. The 'hotel' provided refreshments and shelter.

On the coronation of King Edward in 1902, and George VI in 1937, fires again flared. The town council attended, in full, in 1902, speeches were made, a telegram in Gaelic was sent and toasts were drunk.

The end of the two world wars have also been celebrated, and the coronation of Queen Elizabeth (First of Scotland, Second of England) in 1953.

The Ben was the highest point of a chain of bonfires all over Britain to mark the Royal Family's Silver Jubilee in 1977, and the marriage of Prince Charles to Lady Diana Spencer in July 1981.

The Rev. Alexander Stewart, scientist and historian, wrote in 1894 of a journey of two acquaintances, the Rev. Dr. Macvicar, of Moffat and Sir Walter Trevelyan, to the top of the Ben in June of "some 45 or 50 years ago".

At midday on the summit they were hit by a surprise snow shower. A hissing and crackling noise could be heard and the signs of an electrical discharge could be seen on an umbrella and on the rocks. To the surprise of the party, their beards and hair stood stiff and erect for several minutes as the electrical storm played about them.

Mountain marathons

One of the most noteworthy journeys of modern times was that of Philip Tranter, the mountaineer son of author Nigel Tranter, who traversed the round of the Mamores, the Grey Corries, the Aonachs, Carn Mor Dearg and the Ben in a day and a night in June 1964.

In completing the 18 mountains in 20 hours he climbed 20,000 feet and 36 miles. He reached his first peak, 3007-ft. Mullach nan Coirean, at 5 p.m., and his last, Ben Nevis, at 1 p.m.

Sadly, Philip Tranter was killed in a car crash not long after. He would undoubtedly have become one of Scotland's best-known and skilled climbers.

Philip's round was later repeated by a lady in her forties, Hilary Clark, who took 40 hours. The round has been repeated several times since.

If you think these rounds of the Ben's neighbours are remarkable feats, then look with awe on that performed by Edinburgh-born Charlie Ramsay on July 8, 1978.

He completed the traverse of 23 'Munro' mountains around Ben Nevis in under 24-hours.

It involved 56 miles and a total ascent of 28,000 feet, about the height of Everest.

Charlie carried out his feat to raise funds for the Lochaber Mountain Rescue Association and through sponsorship, gifts and a raffle raised £1,000.

He decided to enlarge on Philip's round of 18 mountains by also going eastward to Loch Treig, around which are another five "Munros" mountains.

In view of the extra distance he knew that navigation would be crucial if he was to be under the 24-hours.

He was an experienced fell-runner, made himself familiar with the route and planned to have drinks and food, fresh socks and T-shirts ready at four checkpoints. There were also to be checkpoints at start and finish, all manned by members of the rescue team.

Volunteer pacers went along and this helped to keep times low and spirits high.

The checkpoints recorded arrival times.

Charlie and his friend, painter Bobby Shields, carried light rucksacks, containing one rain suit, one track suit, one balaclava, one pair of mitts, a torch, first-aid kit, salt tablets, map, whistle, compass and recording sheets.

They left the youth hostel accompanied by two pacers and for a time by Eddie Campbell, the renowned three times winner of the Ben Nevis race.

They first ascended Mullach nan Coirean, the first Munro of Glen Nevis and then pounded steadily on.

They had early mist and rain, but in 12 hours they bagged 12 summits.

Just before Stob a Coire Mheadhoin, west of Loch Treig, Bobby Shields had to drop out with a knee injury. New pacers helped out.

Charlie had successfully sped on througout the night but in the early morning lost precious time through losing the route in mist. As he put it, you can lose a lot of ground in a five-minute burst of downhill running... and then you have to toil back.

On Aonach Beg he made another error, and lost much height. It cost him 40 minutes, but the mist cleared and he speeded up again.

When he reached the Ben's summit he had half an hour to go.

With ten minutes left he could see the youth hostel and the finishing line.

He descended to the footbridge over the Nevis and had 25 yards to go.

With only minutes on the clock he cracked the 24-hours. It is hard to beat as a mountain feat.

If you want to trace Charlie's route on the map, the order of the 23 mountains is — Mullach nan Coirean, Stob Ban, Sgurr a Mhaim, Am Bodach, Stob Coire a Chairn, An Gearanach, Na Gruagaichean, Binnein Mor, Binnein Beag, Sgurr Eilde Mor, then east to Beinn na Lap, north to Cno Dearg and Stob Coire Sgriodain, then west across the Loch Treig dam to Stob a Coire Mheadhoin, Stob Coire Easain, Stob Ban, Stob Coire Claurigh, Stob Coire an Laoigh, Sgurr Choinnich Mor, Aonach Beag,

Aonach Mor, Carn Mor Dearg and Ben Nevis.

There are many tales of grit and press-on determination involving the Ben, but one to marvel at in these days of trains and cars was that of the climbing partnership of William Tough and William Brown in May 1895.

They pioneered climbs in the fine north-east corrie of Lochnagar where their names are commemorated to this day.

They were eager to climb the North-East Buttress of Ben Nevis, as were many of their climbing colleagues at that time, and they selected Queen Victoria's birthday to do it.

They left Edinburgh on the night train to Inverness and reached Kingussie by 3.50 a.m., on a Saturday.

It was raining and misty as they continued on bicycles. A puncture did not deter them. They wheeled for 16 miles to Tulloch station, but could not get a repair done.

Determined to get to the Ben, William Tough then pedalled the remaining bike with their rucksacks, rope, ice-axes and other gear festooned around him and Brown walked or ran alongside.

They reached Fort William by lunchtime, snatched some food and set off for the Ben.

By teatime they had toiled to the foot of the North-East Buttress.

The rocks were wet and they remarked on the number of waterfalls splashing down, but to their relief the rain stopped and the mist lifted and they continued to clamber on.

By 10.5 p.m., they reached the summit and greeted the amazed Observatory staff.

Coffee and an hour's sleep between midnight and 1 a.m., revived them.

They descended in the dark to Fort William and caught the 4 a.m. mail-gig back to Kingussie.

They were back in Edinburgh by early evening, having completed an ascent of Nevis by a quality route new to them and after 40 hours continuous travelling by train, bike, pony-trap, and on foot.

They were happy with their effort, as well they might be, but were later to learn that their ascent of the North-East Buttress had not been the first.

Unknown to them the Hopkinson brothers from England, famous in the late-Victorian annals of British mountaineering, had climbed the buttress three years before.

"Snow For The Royal Wine!"

If you walk to the top of the Ben on a hot summer day with blue skies and perhaps a slight breeze, you might well wonder what all the fuss is about when people talk of snow on the Ben.

But, in fact, snow can fall in any month of the year.

The permanent winter falls normally start in October, but by July the summit plateau is generally clear.

Deep snow lies all-year in large pockets at the foot of the northern and north-east cliffs and gullies and these pockets can be many feet deep.

In past years people went to these snow fields and gullies to collect ice for fish curing. It was carried down in horse panniers.

The "New Statistical Account" of 1845 pointed out that the deep clefts on the north-east side were never without snow.

In winter and spring when the Ben is truly Alpine the gully-mouths and the northern cliff edges are hidden by huge cornices, false edges rather like protruding icing on a cake which can break off carrying the climber with them.

People who have ascended by the pony track must take great care when crossing the summit plateau in spring as the "path" lips the cliff edge.

Dr. John MacCulloch in his book "The Highlands and Western Isles of Scotland" published in 1824, said he had heard that Cameron of Glen Nevis held his lands by the tenure of an unfailing snowball when demanded.

He added, "As this is said in other places also I know not if it is truth or a popular tale."

Seton Gordon, that marvellous naturalist, Scots historian and hillwalker, said there was a local saying that Lochiel would hold his lands so long as there was snow on the Ben. There are similar traditions elsewhere.

The MacIntyres, of Glen Noe, Argyll, are said to have paid their rent with a white calf and a bucket of snow.

They had the high corries of Ben Cruachan nearby.

There is a tradition that the Munros of Foulis held their lands on condition they supplied snow in summer at Holyrood Palace to cool the Royal wine.

The Munros had massive Ben Wyvis nearby which has some deep gullies.

A similar tradition is linked with the Grants of Rothiemurchus who are said to hold their lands provided they supply the sovereign with a bucket of snow when asked for. No problem for them with the Cairngorms at their side.

Ben Nevis in winter can be a fearsome place and good climbers have been caught and have died in avalanches when quick changes of temperature occur.

A mountaineer of the past who said that avalanches on the Ben were rarely so severe as to prevent a buried climber being dug out by his friends would certainly be regarded askance nowadays.

Apart from the danger of burial, avalanches can obviously injure or kill by carrying people downhill over cliffs and buttresses, ledges and boulders. The Ben is beautiful in winter and rightly renowned for the snow and ice climbs it provides for expert mountaineers.

But it needs to be regarded with respect and, additionally, in summer by the tourist-walker.

"Down in the Glen"

The late Seton Gordon, that marvellous naturalist, writer and walker, points out that Glen Nevis and its river had a bad reputation in the old days.

He quotes a 16th-century bard as writing:-

"Glen Nevis, a glen of stones,
A glen where corn ripens late,
A long, wild, waste glen,
With thievish folk of evil habit."

Another tradition says God turned his back on the glen.

Both these sentiments will puzzle many people because the lower sections of the glen are beautiful and fertile.

Many visitors drive to the car park at the head of Glen Nevis and then walk through the Nevis Gorge to the grassy meadows at Steall.

The path through the gorge is rocky but most people who are reasonably nimble can easily manage it.

The birches and pines and the tumbled rocks are a magnificent sight and it is not surprising that there was a public outcry when the North of Scotland Hydro Electric Board proposed to build a 240 ft. high dam across the gorge.

The scheme was later shelved but it could be resurrected again.

Other visitors like to admire the Allt Coire Eoghainn waterslide which falls over 1,000 ft. down the steep sides of Nevis' shoulder Carn Dearg S.W., above the car park.

Don't be tempted to climb the rocks alongside — there have been several accidents.

Allt Coire Eoghainn means the burn of Ewen's Corrie and is pronounced Alt-cawry-Eo-aing (like the English 'owing').

From the Red Burn (descending from the tourist path) round to this waterslide the slopes are no place for the casual walker.

When in the car park you are 450 feet above sea level and the slope goes 4,000 feet to the summit of the Ben at 35 degrees, the longest and steepest hillslope in Britain.

Coire Eoghainn, which bounds the summit plateau on the

south to Carn Dearg S.W., is rarely visited, but some experienced mountaineers do toil up the steep slopes beside the waterslide into the corrie and then go north-east to ultimately go up the boulderly slopes to the Ben's summit.

Glen Nevis has a long pedigree, and has seen much bustle and activity over the centuries.

Nevis Bridge at the mouth of the glen, was once the site in June of a great fair or market when hundreds of cattle were sold. Fort William was also a stopping place for some of the many cattle drives from the Highlands in the 18th and 19th centuries when many beasts went southwards to Crieff and Falkirk for eventual sale.

As you go up the glen look out for a large boulder at the side of the road called Samuel's Stone (Clach Shomairle) or the Wishing Stone or Rolling Stone.

The stone was moved to a new location when the modern road was built and tradition has it that it marks the site of a victory for the people of Glen Nevis, Camerons or MacSorleys, over some enemy. In former times it was said to revolve on its axis and those present at such a time could have the answers to three questions asked of it.

Early in the glen you will see "Cemetery" marked on the map, but there are at least three graveyards in the glen.

At Tom-eas-an-t'slinnean (knoll of the shoulder waterfall), many of the Camerons of Glen Nevis are buried, and the stones go back to 1792 or earlier.

On your way up the glen you pass the modern camping and caravan sites and then Glen Nevis House built on the site of a building which Cameron of Lochiel, Keppoch, and other Jacobite chiefs and leaders occupied during their siege of the fort during the Rising of 1745-6.

The MacSorleys, who pre-dated the Camerons, are said to have had their house on Dun Dighe (the fort of the ditch or moat), to the left of the modern road leading to the Forestry Commission houses.

You will see also that the Ordnance Survey map lists "The Rocking Stone", on the left of the road, set among the Forestry

Commission trees, and not long past the Youth Hostel.

In Gaelic, it is Clach-an-turramain and despite its size it could be rocked on its base. Older Fort William inhabitants remember doing that, but it now appears to be set firm.

Traces of ancient fortifications can be seen on a knoll, about half-a-mile beyond Glen Nevis house. On it are the remains of a vitrified fort, dating to around 500 B.C. and known locally as Dun Dearduil. It is said to be one of a chain that links the east and west coasts.

Just opposite (on the left of the road) is another old graveyard at Achnacon (Field of the Dogs), thought to be an earlier burial ground of the Camerons.

At Achriabhach — a name visitors enjoy saying (it means the brindled field) and at Achnacon there are the remains of the old townships of people evicted or "moved" during the Clearances.

Just past Achriabhach and close to the tumbled boulders and crags at Polldubh (black pool) the road turns sharply, crosses the Nevis, and the scenery becomes much wilder.

The crags at Polldubh provides excellent rock-climbing and the visitor can often watch local climbers and visitors in action.

The rocks are also used for mountain-rescue stretcher-lowering practice purposes. The writer recalls, as a guest of the R.A.F. Kinloss team, being lowered in a stretcher down "Sheep-Fank Wall" and some other climbs, and the alarm on the face of the R.A.C. "patient" when the positions were reversed. Once the R.A.F. "patient" had been strapped in and couldn't move, the writer was invited to guide the stretcher down the cliff, an invitation eagerly accepted and safely accomplished but the patient didn't enjoy it too much.

The road passes between two prominent pine trees and ends at the car park.

Don't be tempted to clamber over to the dark entrance to Samuel's Cave, opposite the car park. It's not worth it. The rocks are often wet and greasy, and it can be a dangerous jaunt. Just look from afar.

Once through the Gorge you arrive at the mountaineering hut at Steall, reached over a bridge of three wires. Entry is by advance permission only and the hut is locked.

Steall means a spout or torrent and is pronounced stale or s-ch-owl, as in owl.

The beautiful Steall waterfall is on the lowest cliff of Sgurr a Mhaim and is 350 feet high.

It is one of the three biggest in Scotland (the others are the Falls of Glomach, Kintail, 350 feet, and the remote Eas a Chual Aluinn, in Sutherland., 658 ft.).

Steall is a beautiful place but there is a sombre atmosphere about it which I tended to put down to its bowl-like shape and steep, over-shadowing mountains and, perhaps, the nearness of the gorge.

There is also a sad tale attached to this house which now rings to the laughter and banter of hillwalkers and rock-climbers.

Long ago the house was used by a stalker and his family.

They had a small girl of three who one day, running to meet her father when he returned from the hill, tripped and fell into the Nevis which was then in spate.

Before her father could reach her she was swept away. Her body was later recovered from one of the deep pools in the gorge.

The family left the house not long after, never to return.

"The Year of Miracles"

The huge bulk of Ben Nevis and its neighbours have seen many warring armies but probably none more valiant than the one which vanished amid the January storms of 1645.

The Civil War was raging in England as Charles I struggled to save his crown, the war popularly known as that between Cavaliers and Roundheads.

In Scotland, the linked Wars of the Covenant were taking place. Because of the neglect of Scottish history in Scottish schools, the events here are not so well know as they should be but they include a military campaign which is considered so brilliant that it is closely studied to this day.

The Ben and its neighbouring hills were to be of great tactical significance in this campaign.

The leaders were a slim, scholarly, gentle courtier-soldier who has become one of the most revered figures in Scottish history, James Graham, Marquis of Montrose, and his ally, Alasdair MacColla, popularly known as Colkitto MacDonald, the strapping and fearsome war leader of the clan Donald and the clan's Ulstermen who, with other Irishmen, joined their kinsmen and allies in Scotland for the cause of the King, for their religious beliefs, for booty, for the glory of clan Donald and — some would say — for the sheer zest of it all.

James Graham originally joined the Covenanters but he became alienated by extremists and self-seekers. He opposed Scottish intervention in the English civil war and ultimately turned against the Covenanters.

With a handful of followers he endeavoured to win Scotland for Charles I.

Alexander or Alastair MacDonald, (later to be known as Major General Sir Alexander MacDonald) was born on the island of Colonsay, south of Mull. He was given the nick name Coitach or Left-handed (slurred into Colkitto), and war was his profession and his delight. He is credited with creating the Highland charge which was a controlled affair of great power and planned formation.

Montrose is traditionally judged to be the genius behind the

ı Nevis in winter raiment, from Corpach.

ı Nevis in winter raiment seen across Loch Eil.

The river Nevis flows through the meadows of Steall, upper Glen Nevis.

campaign they were to conduct, but some modern historians persuasively argue that the credit should go to Colkitto, his second-in-command.

If you want the flavour of the period, and a good read as well in a fairly popular format, get hold of Maurice Walsh's novel "And No Quarter".

Montrose arrived back in Scotland just in time because Colkitto and his men were in difficulties.

They found no armies to greet them in Scotland and were forced to live on what they could scrounge. They had 'lifted' cattle from the Athole clans and from their neighbours.

The Camerons and Stewarts were ready for throat-cutting, but Montrose ended the tensions. He brought them all together, outlined his plans and as Clan Campbell was prominent in the ranks of the Covenanting armies, Colkitto's Irish and the Stewarts, Camerons and Macdonalds had little difficulty in joining forces against their hated enemies.

It was a small army of a few thousands but it was formidable.

It is sometimes thought nowadays that the Clansmen were an untidy rabble, more interested in plunder than skilled warfare, a bunch of unruly brigands whose wild charge could be broken by disciplined troops.

(It is true that the Jacobite charge at Culloden in 1746 was destroyed by Hanoverian soldiers but there were complicating circumstances of bad leadership, hunger, exhaustion, and irresolution).

They were men accustomed to holding their lands by the sword. They considered arms an honourable profession, and their leaders studied war with great success.

With much of the Highlands given over to cattle, reiving and rescuing cattle was a fairly regular occurrence.

Men were accustomed to 'sleeping rough', to hardship, to ambush and evasion. They could skilfully place sentinels and patrols, and equally skilfully dodge them. They could march or trot huge distances. The care and use of their weapons, sword, dirk, targe, musket and pistols, were second-nature. They were brave and hardy.

Montrose, "Colkitto" and their men took to the hills.

Like the North American Indian, they knew the wild life of their own hills and glens, could live off the land, travel at night, and fade into the landscape.

There have possibly been no other soldiers like them, but they needed leadership that understood them and their way of life.

Montrose and Colkitto faced more than one army, and they gained an initial breathing space by routing a Covenant army at Tippermuir, near Perth, in front of the alarmed gaze of the townspeople who had come to watch the Highlanders and Irish being slaughtered.

They fought some cunning withdrawals, sacked Aberdeen and then — urged on by Colkitto — crossed Scotland to hit the Clan Campbell capital of Inveraray, at Loch Fyne. The Marquis of Argyle escaped in a boat, and that disgrace has not been forgotten yet.

In the Highland saying, the heather was o'er the gale. (Heather is the badge of Clan Donald. Gale (bog myrtle) is that of the Campbells).

Montrose's men lived well and snugly at Inveraray in the winter weeks and then, with armies closing in on them, pulled out and made their way to Loch Ness-side, near the present-day Fort Augustus (then called Kilcumin).

Here they faced a new threat. The Earl of Seaforth was at Inverness with 5,000 men and was expected to move down the Great Glen towards them.

Montrose's army was reduced to about 1,500 men, mainly Colkitto's plus some Macdonalds, Stewarts, McGregors, McLeans and others.

Many had temporarily gone home to dump the booty taken from Inveraray and it was known they would return when they could. But the absentees did include some of the best fighting soldiers from the Macdonalds of Clanranald and the men of Athole.

Montrose and Colkitto must have been perturbed when a messenger arrived with urgent news.

Over 3,000 Campbells, plus some Lowland levies, were at Inverlochy (on the fringe of present-day Fort William). They were sending out parties to burn the Cameron, Stewart and Macdonald homesteads in revenge for the sacking of Inveraray, and they were panting to get at the throats of Montrose's army.

The Great Glen, where the present-day Caledonian Canal links the lochs, is like a sword-cut through the hills.

Imagine Montrose's army about halfway along. From the tip of the blade Seaforth is preparing to move down.

From the hilt come the Campbells.

There is no escape to the west where there is only the coast. To the east, another Covenanting army under General Baillie is moving towards Montrose's men.

Three armies threaten sooner or later, and all around are the Highland hills, bleak and snow-covered, inhospitable and shelterless.

All this was pondered by Montrose and Colkitto as they listened to the breathless messenger, Ian Lom, the famous bard of Keppoch, as he told his news of the Campbells approach.

On Friday, January 31, Montrose and Colkitto vanished. They took to the hills.

Campbell and Seaforth scouts found an empty glen as they probed towards one another.

Montrose's army had little food, only oatmeal mixed with melting snow, but they had men who knew Ben Nevis and its surrounding hills.

They planned to work their way back to Inverlochy by hill routes and surprise the Campbells. They would fight their strongest enemy first.

Historians differ on the route the army took but it is now thought unlikely they crossed as far over as Glen Nevis and came down that glen to Inverlochy.

Have a look at the Ordnance Survey map — one theory goes that they went up the little River Tarff, crossing above Cullachy, then parallel to the present-day canal until the Calder Burn above Aberchalder Lodge, then up the burn and turning south up the Alt-nan-Larach till the headwaters of the Turritt were reached, then southwest into Glen Roy along the so-called "Parallel Roads".

Ahead lay the Ben and its foothills.

Anyone who knows Scottish hills in winter will marvel at that march of men with little food, tugging their plaids close, their weapons hung around them as they waded through the hill snow.

Neil Munro in his historical novel "John Splendid" (Blackwoods) draws a graphic picture of that terrible journey, the strung-out army like ants on a white sheet.

Those who wore trews (trousers) found their soaking clothes freezing to their legs. Those who wore the kilt were at least still supple.

He writes; "At the head of Glen Roy, the Macdonalds, who had lost their bauchles or brogues in the pass, started to a trot ...long, lank hounds, they took to the road like deer, their lips purple with the cold, their faces pinched to the aspect of the wolf, their targets (shields) and muskets clattering about them. 'There are Campbells to slay and suppers to eat', the Major-General (Colkitto) had said. It would have given his most spiritless followers the pith to run till morning across a strand of rock and pebble. They knew no tiring, they seemingly felt no pain in their torn and bleeding feet, but put mile after mile below them".

From Roy bridge to Iverlochy is only 13 miles but Montrose and Colkitto wanted a surprise circuit.

They forded the river Spean near Corriechoille, and wended a secretive way by the old townships of Kilchonate and Leanachan, and were at the foot of the Ben's shoulder of Meall an t-Suidhe before dark.

They could see the tower of ancient Inverlochy Castle, and the Campbells moving around their camp, cooking, eating and relaxing.

Sentries saw them but the Campbells concluded they were only raiders or foraging parties.

Montrose's men lay out all night, in freezing temperatures and with no food, and at dawn on February 2 the pipes told the stupefied Campbells that an entire army was preparing to attack.

The Marquis of Argyll had injured his shoulder and was persuaded to stay on board a galley offshore.

Campbell of Auchinbrek, with experience of foreign wars, took command. He stationed the main body of Campbells in the centre and put the lowland troops on the wings, bolstered by some Campbells.

Highlander against Lowlander in the Montrose campaigns.

There was a strong reserve force, too, with some cannon.

Unfortunately for the Campbells they had a good number of their men missing, out scouring the glens for Montrose's men and taking their revenge for Inveraray.

Nevertheless, they still outnumbered Montrose's army by about 1,000.

Colkitto led the Irish on the right wing, his friend Manus O'Cahan (later to be executed after the battle of Philiphaugh) led the left. Montrose led the centre, composed of men from Athole, the Stewarts of Appin, MacIans from Glen Coe and the Camerons.

The remnants of Clanranald and Macdonalds of Glengarry were in the second line.

The Irish on the wings charged the hurriedly assembled Lowland soldiers. Just before the point of impact they fired their pistols and muskets, and then the roaring men crashed into the confused and smoke-ridden ranks who had never before faced a Gaelic charge.

The soldiers broke and fled.

Montrose's men then did the same to the Campbell centre, which with its flanks gone, was forced back on its reserve which also cracked.

The Campbell clansmen fought valiantly but in time they too were cut into groups and eventually broke.

There was little quarter. The very tide ran red and all over Lochaber, Appin,Glen Garry and Glen Coe the exultant word went out and men got out their weapons for the joyful purpose of disposing of Campbell fugitives.

Auchinbrek was among the slain.

Ian Lom, Keppoch's bard, who had brought the news of the Campbells arival at Inverlochy to Montrose and Colkitto, wrote an epic poem glorying in the victory.

"Through the land of my fathers the Campbells have come,
The flames of their foray enveloped my home;
Broad Keppoch in ruin is left to deplore,
And my country is waste from the hill to the shore,
Be it so! By St. Mary, there's comfort in store.

Though the braes of Lochaber a desert he made,
And Glen Roy may be lost to the plough and the spade,
Though the bones of my kindred, unhonourd, unurned,
Mark the desolate path where the Campbells have burned —
Be it so! From that foray they never returned."

Ahead lay more brilliant tactical marching and victories at Auldearn and Alford in the north-east and at Kilsyth. But tragedy eventually came.

When Colkitto was away on some ploy of his own, Montrose's reduced force were surprised at Philiphaugh, near Selkirk, in September 1645, and routed. The captured were executed, as were their womenfolk and children. Montrose escaped but was later captured.

On May 21, 1650, Montrose was taken to Edinburgh and publicly hanged. (Colkitto later died in Ireland in a way he would have wished, sword in hand. A Gaelic proverb says 'Better a swift death in battle than a lingering one in bed".

Watching Montrose go to his death was his enemy, the Marquis of Argyll.

Five years before he had watched from a galley moored offshore at Inverlochy as his army was cut to pieces by Montrose and Colkitto's men after their magnificent march around the foothills of the Ben in a campaign which came to be called the year of miracles.

"The Sleeping Giants of Samuel's Cave"

Near the head of Glen Nevis the road passes closely between two prominent trees, and once one reaches the car park one can see across the river a jumble of large boulders, backed by steep grass and heather.

In this wild section of the glen is a damp and hidden fissure known as Samuel's Cave.

Some people visit it — although it is often wet and unpleasant — and they are following in the footsteps of shadowy and real figures from the past.

Exactly who the renowned Samuel was is a matter for conjecture and dispute, but the glen was originally the home of the MacSorleys, of the race of Somerled (Samuel) the Red, and who later became part of Clan Cameron and who took their name.

The entrance is narrow and the visitor has to stoop. There is an initial, airy cave, which leads into an inner recess.

The height varies from six to fifteen feet, the breadth about ten, and the length about thirty.

The floor slopes and two passages lead off to other corners. One descends ten feet and the other goes up above the roof of the main cavern.

It is said the cave was once the home of the mighty fianna, the ancient heroes and giants of Gaelic mythology.

It was here they fell asleep and tradition has it that a horn blown for the third time will bring them to their feet once more.

Legend tells that a hunter exploring the cave found a horn in the entrance chamber and blew it. To his astonishment, the cave was suddenly full of huge men who blinked sleepily at him.

He blew again and they raised themselves on to their elbows, and began to reach for their gigantic swords and spears.

The hunter dropped the horn and fled, and no third blast was ever uttered.

Other stories tell of one of the cave's passages running for five miles (which it doesn't) and that a band of Camerons on a reiving (cattle rustling) expedition were pursued into it. Their hunters heard the sound of the pipes, faintly, from within the cave and are

He blew again... and they reached for their gigantic swords.

said to have then abandoned the hunt as the Camerons had clearly escaped by another exit.

Another Highland story tells of a piper and his friends who sheltered in the cave and who found the entrance blocked by a fierce wolf. The piper played his pipes and found that the wolf seemed hypnotised by the music.

She didn't attack them, but nor did she let them out and it is said they descended into the darkness, never again to reappear, with the sounds of the pipes getting fainter and fainter.

During a time of Clan wars, and land disputes, the MacSorleys and representatives of Clan Chattan held a peace-making conference in Glen Nevis.

When they were parting, a piper played the Camerons' war-tune, and the Clan Chattan delegation was deeply insulted. They decided to return later and re-pay the insult.

At dead of night they fell on the sleeping Camerons. All were massacred, the story goes, except the chief's young son, called Somerled, (Samuel) who was grabbed by a clansman, Iain MacDhon 'ic Raoil, and hurried to safety.

Title deeds to the glen lands and a silver spoon were the only other objects the rescuer had time to snatch up and remove.

He took the child to Samuel's Cave and some story-tellers claim that is why it is called Samuel's Cave to this day.

The faithful Iain looked after the boy in the cave. For fear that the Clan Chattan men would return he even hid his secret from his wife.

Unfortunately, a dog he had with him attracted his wife to the cave, and he was forced to flee Lochaber with the boy as others, hungry for Cameron land, sought to eliminate him.

Many years later Iain returned disguised as a beggar.

He went to a house called Inverlair where an aunt of Somerled resided.

He begged for food for the boy and the silver spoon was used to eat it.

The stupefied aunt recognised it, and demanded an explanation.

The whole story came out, and the chief of the Camerons, Lochiel, was told. Safety was guaranteed.

One of the soldiers slit her plaid open with his sword.

He held a conference of the whole clan, and Somerled — now 17 — was recognised as the rightful successor of the lands of Glen Nevis.

Samuel's cave, too, was a refuge for Mrs. Cameron of Glen Nevis House who fled there when the troops of the Duke of Cumberland plundered the glen after Prince Charles Edward Stuart's Jacobite Army was defeated at Culloden in 1746.

It was from Glen Nevis House in the period immediately before Culloden that the Camerons' chief, Lochiel, and the neighbouring chief of the Macdonnells of Keppoch issued a declaration condemning the Campbells for their part in the burning of homes, the eviction of women and children and the stealing and maiming of cattle and livestock by the Hanoverian soldiers and militia.

The statement urged that war should not be made on women and children, and stressed the chiefs' intention of ensuring redress in battle.

However, retribution was not to be. Keppoch fell at Culloden and Lochiel was wounded and had to go into hiding.

When the Redcoats were sacking the lands of the Jacobite clans, Mrs. Cameron of Glen Nevis hid her family's most treasured possessions, and then fled to Samuel's cave.

She was found there by the Redcoats and questioned.

Highland tradition says she was hugging her plaid close to her body, and that one of the soldiers, thinking she was hiding money or jewellery, slit it open with his sword.

He found nothing but her baby son, Ewan.

The sword nicked Ewan's neck and left him with a scar which remained for life.

"The Witch who Saved a Clan Chief"

Long, long ago when the winter snows fell on Ben Nevis and the other hills of Lochaber, and the evenings were dark and the nights noisy with gales and storms, the people would sometimes gather in one another's houses and hold ceilidhs.

They sang songs of heroic battles, of lost causes and distant campaigns, of romance and love, and of the beauties of the hills and glens of their native place.

Their stone and turf houses were not large but they were snug and hardy, and there was room for a family and a few friends to gather and huddle round a peat fire.

In the light of the embers, or of a flickering fir or rush candle, they told stories of water-horses and witches, of strange vows and fairy mounds, of goblins and the second sight. They told such stories, too, at the spring shielings, when the people took their cattle to the fresh grass of the glens and on to the moors, where they lived in temporary houses for most of the summer.

And one tale they told was of the quarrel between Locheil, Chief of Clan Cameron, and the Earl of Atholl over the boundaries of their land, and how the Gormshuil, or Gormla, the Witch of Moy, came to Locheil's rescue.

The Gormshuil (pronounced Gormhool) was famous in the legends of Clan Cameron, and she lived not far from Achnacarry where Locheil had his home. She is said to have encouraged the witches of the island of Mull to deal with the storm-battered ships of the Spanish Armada.

Our story concerns the Lochan a' Chlaidheimh (The Little Loch of the Sword), sited to the east of the Blackwater Reservoir and a few miles north-west of present-day Rannoch Station.

You can see the lochan from the train en route to Fort William or on your way south.

The boundary or march between the Cameron lands in east Lochaber and the Earl of Atholl's lands of Rannoch was a matter of dispute. Both chiefs laid claim to the hill-grazings of Aird-Raineach, part of Beinn a Bhreac and the meadows of the Black Water.

They negotiated with one another, and their tempers ran so high that blows were exchanged.

Their men, too, were reaching for sword and dirk when Locheil and Atholl calmed them down, and stiffly parted from one another.

But before they left Atholl said to Locheil: "You and I should meet alone and try to settle which of us has the better right to the land of Aird-raineach. It would be best not to have our men with us so that if we do not agree again we will not have a fight.

"If you are willing to meet again at Aird-raineach without your men I am willing to do the same.

"We shall meet and reason the case, with justice, between ourselves and each shall plead his cause with civility.

"While we use civil language to one another we shall not grow wrathful. If there is no anger there will not be fighting. If there is no fighting blood shall not be shed".

Lochiel pondered this and then said: "I am willing to meet you without any person but my piper being present.

"I want my piper to be there because I like to have someone who will listen to what is said so that he can remind me of it again."

The Earl of Atholl agreed to this, and said he would bring his piper as well.

Both chiefs then marched home with their men, and word spread among their clan people of the pact they had made.

When the day came Lochiel rose early to go to the meeting. He wore his best tartan, set his chief's eagle feather at a proud angle in his bonnet and ensured his piper also looked trim and smart.

They set out on their journey in the early hours of the morning and to their surprise an old woman appeared at the side of the track and greeted them.

It was the witch Gormla. Her sudden appearance so startled Lochiel that he spoke brusquely to her.

"What are you doing here so early in the morning? Why have you made certain you are the first person to greet me?"

Gormla slowly smiled and said: "And what great business has sent you so early on the road, and why are you so angry? Do you think I am a bad omen?"

Lochiel told her about the pact he had made, and told her he

Gormla the witch asked: "Do you think I am a bad omen?"

was in a hurry as it was many miles from Achnacarry to the Aird Raineach.

Gormla looked very perturbed.

"But Lochiel, where are your warriors? Do not trust the Earl of Atholl. Please, please take my advice," she pleaded.

"Go back and get your best men. Take them with you to your meeting and leave them in hiding behind a hill.

"Arrange a sign so that if danger threatens they can hurry to your aid. Take three score and five of your best warriors.

"It would be a wise precaution. If nothing goes wrong, then the Earl of Atholl need never know you had your men with you."

Lochiel agreed to what she said, and Gormla bid him farewell and set off home.

Lochiel hurriedly gathered together a band of 65 of his best men, and set out again on his journey.

When he reached the area of Aird-Raineach he hid his men behind a hill and told them to stay quiet.

"If you hear my piper play, look carefully to see what is happening.

"If you see the gray side of my cloak out it shall be a sign that the Earl of Atholl and I have agreed. Stay hidden.

"But if you see my red lining, then I shall be in danger. Come running, and ready to fight."

Lochiel and his piper then went forward to a small mound where the Earl of Atholl stood with his piper behind him.

Both chiefs saluted one another, shook hands and got down to discussing who was the rightful owner of Aird Raineach.

But they could not agree, and tempers flared again.

Suddenly, Atholl flung off his cloak. It, too, was a planned sign because men bearing arms stood up among the heather, and hurried to his side.

Lochiel, knowing he probably had only minutes to live, tried to gain time.

"Who are these men?", he asked.

The Earl answered: "These are some of the Atholl ewes (female sheep) coming to eat the first crop of Lochaber."

Lochiel took off his cloak, turned it round so the red-lining showed, and nonchalantly wrapped it round himself again. His piper struck up a tune.

The hidden Camerons looked to see what was happening. They saw the red lining, and hurried to Lochiel's aid. "Who are they?", asked the Earl. Lochiel replied: "These are some of the Lochaber dogs coming to chase away the Atholl ewes."

Both chiefs drew their swords, and aimed blows at one another.

Their men charged forward, dirk and targe (shield) at the ready, and met in a ferocious, yelling melee.

But the Camerons were more numerous and got the upper hand. Atholl's men were killed or fled. The Earl was taken prisoner, and later formally resigned his claim to the land.

And the Camerons are thought to have made a new pipe tune, and created a new rallying cry from that day: "Sons of dogs, come here and get flesh."

Throughout all Lochaber, the fame of Gormla spread and Locheil paid her many tributes.

But there was to be yet another twist to this tale.

As a pledge of his good faith, the Earl of Atholl kissed his sword and threw it into the lochan on the boundary of the disputed land.

To this day the lochan is called Lochan a Chlaidheimh (the Little Loch of the Sword), is pronounced Lochun uh Ch (as in loch) Chlaye-uhr and the old county boundary of Inverness-shire and Perthshire ran through it.

In 1826, when some men were fishing there, they found an old rusty broadsword. It was taken to the parish Minister of Kilmonivaig.

Later, as word spread, a deputation of 12 Camerons requested that the sword be given to them, and they then threw it back into the loch where it still lies.

"Terror of the Talking Cats"

When it became time to tell stories around the winter fires, there was one tale which made the little children cry out in fear and put their hands over their ears.

Even the grown-ups did not like it very much for it is a truly horrible story. It is very old, and has several versions.

It concerned the witch of Moy, Gormshuil (or Gormla) herself, the same witch who saved Lochiel from treachery when he went to meet the Earl of Atholl to discuss how they should settle a boundary dispute.

One version says the Cameron chief involved in this story was Ailean nan Creach, but another says it was Ewen MacAllan. The story goes back at least as far as the 16th century so we will simply call the chief by his land title, Lochiel, which is, after all, the Highland custom.

Now, Lochiel was a great fighter and an ambitious man. He enlarged the lands owned by the Camerons, and he launched seven expeditions into other areas and he took these lands by conquest.

But as he grew older he began to reflect on the men he had killed, the houses he had burned and the cattle he had stolen, and he was filled with sorrow and remorse.

His eldest son, Donald, who was a youth of many talents, manly, strong, brave and clever, fell ill of a mysterious disease and died.

This greatly added to Lochiel's grief and he consulted Gormshuil about how he could atone for the sins he had committed and the evil he had done.

Gormshuil told him to build a Tigh Gairm (A House of Invocation or Prayer) and when that was done he would be told what to do next.

So Lochiel had a house of turf and wattles built beside the River Lochy and he waited there for Gormshuil's instructions.

She told him that he was to call one servant to wait with him and he was to light a huge fire.

He was also to take a cat with him.

He was to run a spit (a spike for cooking) through the cat while still keeping it alive and the servant was then to roast the cat over the fire.

Lochiel was ordered to guard the door against anyone trying to enter, and he would then be given further instructions.

The screeches of the cat could be heard a long way off, and a very strange thing happened.

From all around other cats came to the hut, their eyes and teeth gleaming, their claws out, all looking large and menacing and ferocious.

They gathered round the door, snarling and spitting and they seemed to grow until they were much larger than the wild cat of the hills.

They could speak as well and they demanded to be allowed into the hut and that the roasting cat be released. The threatened to tear Lochiel to pieces unless he freed the cat, but he kept them back with his sword.

He shouted to his servant: "Whatever you hear or see, turn the spit and roast the cat."

The mob of cats outside the door skirled and screeched but Lochiel drove them back.

Then a huge black cat, the King of the Cats, came forward and told the rest to be silent.

The awful clamour ended and a deathly hush fell.

The King of the Cats came near to Lochiel and asked him to stop roasting the cat in the hut.

Lochiel replied, "I will let it go if you tell me how I can gain forgiveness for all the terrible deeds I have done."

The King of the Cats said he had to build seven churches to atone for his seven conquering expeditions.

Lochiel then released the cat and it dashed out of the door and leaped into a pool in the River Lochy.

This pool, near Torcastle, is still known as Poll a' Chait (The Cat Pool).

All the other cats also leaped into the river and were carried downstream. They returned to their normal size and went back to their own homes.

The King of the Cats ordered Lochiel to stop the roasting.

Lochiel then returned to his house and soon gave instructions that seven churches were to be built on his own lands or where he had influence or friends.

They were built at Kilmallie, Kildonan, Cill a' Choireil in Brae Lochaber (Roy Bridge), Kilchoan in Knoydart, Arisaig, Morven and Kilkillen, Loch Laggan.

All now have gone except for mounds, and only the Cat's Pool remains to tell of the days when Lochiel met the King of the Cats and the witch of Moy played her part in the building of the seven churches.

(But as well as eerie tales the people told, with relish, stories of courage in battle. The next tale is such a one...)

Death fight of the clansmen

The Camerons were always a race of warriors, well able to hold their lands by the strength of their sword-arm, and with a justifiable pride in their own way of life.

They were angered and shaken in 1650 when General Monk, Cromwell's Governor in Scotland, built a fort right in the middle of their own territory as part of a number of such strongholds designed to subdue the Highland chiefs who were Royalist in their sympathies.

General Monk built his first fort by stealth, landing troops on the shores of Loch Linnhe near where the River Nevis enters the loch and hurriedly erecting 'walls' of turf and makeshift barricades.

Many of the Cameron clansmen, under their chief, Sir Ewen Cameron of Lochiel, who was then aged about 25, were far away engaged in other battles.

When they returned they were taken aback at this stronghold in their midst, and they determined to smoke it out.

Lochiel knew that the soldiers frequently went to Achdalieu, on the shores of Loch Eil, to cut timber to build up the fort, and he carefully noted their movements.

One day, he hid 50 of his best men among the trees. The soldiers greatly outnumbered them, but when the soldiers were busy felling trees the Camerons rushed upon them, firing their muskets and then following it up with a hail of arrows.

The soldiers also fired their muskets but their clumsy bayonets were no match for the Camerons and they fell back towards the shore.

The Camerons cut them down with their broadswords and dirks.

In the confusion of the hand-to-hand fighting Lochiel got cut off from his men and was engaged in single combat with a burly soldier.

The struggle was long and desperate, and both men used their swords cleverly but neither could get an advantage over the other.

The soldier was stronger and bigger, but Lochiel was more nimble, and they both grew breathless with thrust and parry.

Suddenly, with a quick twist of his wrist, Lochiel managed to prise the sword out of his opponent's hand but before he could hack him down the soldier leaped on him.

Both fell to the ground and a frenzied wrestling match took place.

They struggled and rolled over with neither being able to get the upper hand until they tumbled down the banks of a dried-up burn.

They lay there panting, each so exhausted that neither could lift a hand. But Lochiel had been pinned underneath in the fall and could not move.

When the soldier got his breath back he loosened his hold slightly to get at his dagger which was at his waist. That gave Lochiel his chance. In desperation, he lunged up grabbed the soldier by the collar and tore out a piece of the man's throat with his teeth.

He was then able to throw him off and despatch him with his dirk.

In later years the clansmen jocularly quoted Lochiel as saying it was the sweetest mouthful he had ever tasted.

Lochiel also had another escape when a soldier fired at him from a boat but his foster-brother bravely threw himself in front of Lochiel and stopped the bullet with his own body.

Legend has it that there was a sequel to this incident.

Lochiel was in London many years later and went to the barbers before going to Court.

The barber conversed with him and said, "You are from the north, sir?"

Lochiel replied that indeed he was, and asked the barber if he knew anyone from these parts.

The barber is said to have replied, "No, nor do I wish to. One of them tore the throat out of my father and I only wish I had the fellow's throat as near me now as yours is."

The Camerons attacked other parties of soldiers, but eventually a truce was agreed and the clansmen and the soldiers ultimately became friends.

The killings and the affair of the bitten throat were temporarily forgotten.

Lochiel and the soldier tumbled down the banks of a burn.

But later generations recalled them and they were told with pride around many a winter fire and at many a ceilidh.

Author's notes
(March, 1986)

In the "Down in the Glen" section, the reference to the R.A.C. should of course read R.A.F. In "Year of the Miracles" I mention the novel *And No Quarter* as giving a good flavour of the Covenanting period. The reader may also find David Stevenson's *Alasdair Mac Colla and the Highland Problem of the 17th Century* of interest. This is the definitive work of the period and is published by John Donald, Edinburgh. The reference on page six of this chapter to Colkitto is an error and should read Montrose.

Update to the "Great Race" chapter: in 1984 Kendal gardener Kenneth Stewart set up a new record of one hour, 25 minutes, 34 seconds, beating by one second the time set in 1983 by J Wild, Cumberland.

Hills mentioned in the book with an a in the title would in most cases have an apostrophe after this letter.